COLLABORATE
FOR
SUCCESS

THE SINGLE MOST POWERFUL MARKETING STRATEGY FOR LOW COST LEADS & MAJOR PROFIT

Gilad Segev

Collaborate for Success:
The Single Most Powerful Marketing Strategy For Low Cost Leads & Major Profit
www.Collaboratesuccess.com
Copyright © 2021 Gilad Segev

Cover design: Studio LeniGraphics
Illustrations: Dana Bender

ISBN: 979-8529564882

All rights reserved. No portion of this book may be reproduced mechanically, electronically, or by any other means, including photocopying, without permission of the publisher or author except in the case of brief quotations embodied in critical articles and reviews. It is illegal to copy this book, post it to a website, or distribute it by any other means without permission from the publisher or author.

Limits of Liability and Disclaimer of Warranty
The author and publisher shall not be liable for your misuse of the enclosed material. This book is strictly for informational and educational purposes only.

Warning – Disclaimer
The purpose of this book is to educate and entertain. The author and/or publisher do not guarantee that anyone following these techniques, suggestions, tips, ideas, or strategies will become successful. The author and/or publisher shall have neither liability nor responsibility to anyone with respect to any loss or damage caused, or alleged to be caused, directly or indirectly by the information contained in this book.

Publisher
10-10-10 Publishing
Markham, ON   Canada

Printed in Canada and the United States of America

WHAT WORLD LEADING ENTREPRENEURS ARE SAYING ABOUT THIS BOOK….

"Collaborations are one of the most significant strategies a company can use to grow and make a bigger impact in the world. We have used them continuously for over 2 decades at our 7 and 8 figure companies. Gilad can help you get the strategies and mindset you need to get on top of the collaborations you need to grow!"

Kane Minkus (From Kane & Alessia) – 3X Bestselling Author, Founder of Industry Rockstar, Serial Entrepreneur & International Speaker

"Partnerships and collaborations are vital tools for any business of any size. In this book, Gilad provides the most essential step by step practical guide for setting a WIN/WIN relationship between two small businesses, leading them in the business path for growth."

Kevin Harrington – Original Shark on ABC's *SharkTank,* Bestselling Author, Known as the $6 Billion Man, Inventor of the Infomercial *As Seen On TV*

Collaborate for Success

"In a business world that generates more and more complexity daily, it's great to have a guide that can make sense of it all. It's refreshing to know that even today, there are some proven and time tested strategies that can cut through the clutter to short-cut your route to success. Gilad's book has provided clear and easy to understand guidance on one of the most powerful strategies in business. This book is filled with many profound insights, and if you want accelerate your progress, you will learn to master the art of collaboration. Start here."

Kevin Paetz – Serial Entrepreneur, International Speaker, Global Strategist and Advisor to CEOs

"Our GOALS can only be reached through a vehicle of a PLAN, in which we must fervently believe, and upon which we must vigorously act. There is no other route to SUCCESS."
– Pablo Picasso

*To my beloved parents,
for their inequivalent support
and life inspiration.*

*To my beloved children: Shaked, Tomer and Chen,
each a leader in their own right, and each independently
living a life of dedication and contribution.*

PREFACE

Dear entrepreneur and marketing manager, this book is not your conventional theoretical teaching book. The purpose of this book is to get your business moving much faster, and my goal is to sum up many years of negotiation experience into this short guide.

This book is designed to provide information that the author believes to be accurate on the subject matter it covers, but it is sold with the understanding that the author is not offering individualized advice tailored to any specific person or business.

The purpose of this book is to provide you with short, step-by-step "how-to" procedures, and a dummy-proof path to success. All you need to do is embed these steps into your day-to-day business activities so that you will feel the difference in your bank account within a short period of time.

Please be aware that you may feel the need to go over some sections of the book more than once. This is to be expected, and once you get that urge, you may commend yourself for really embedding these steps into your business.

> *"Success consists of going from failure to failure without loss of enthusiasm."*
> – Winston Churchill

CONTENTS

INTRODUCTION xiii
FOREWORD xvii

Chapter 1: KNOWING YOUR TARGET AND SETTING GOALS 1
Chapter 2: SET YOUR MISSIONS AND OBJECTIVES. 19
Chapter 3: SET MUTUAL AGREED BASSLINE 35
Chapter 4: COMMUNICATION TOOLS FOR SUCCESS 49
Chapter 5: AGREEMENT ON FACTS 63
Chapter 6: COMMUNICATING TOWARDS AGREEMENT.............75
Chapter 7: SUGGEST THE COLLABORATION...............................93
Chapter 8: CLOSE THE DEAL..109
Chapter 9: THE NETWORKING WAY TO CLIENTS......................131
Chapter 10: LASERPOINT YOUR CLIENT TO INCREASE
            YOUR PROFITS..147

ACKNOWLEDGMENTS 169
ABOUT THE AUTHOR 173
BONUSES AND TOOLS..175

Special Bonuses available at
www.CollaborateSuccess.com

INTRODUCTION

This straight to the point book on collaborations, written from an entrepreneur for other entrepreneurs, couldn't be more timely. The insights and recommendations are timeless. Small business owners, entrepreneurs and even marketing managers should read it and take what it says to heart.

Never has the marketing world experienced such turbulent times. Following the social media domination taking all as captives in its grip, this book finally gives you solutions and alternatives to reclaim your power. Gilad Segev aptly points out that placing all marketing efforts in the same basket may turn out to be an expensive path. A path that may cost the organization not only money but also its existence.

What helps make the potential of this volume so influential is that the author is upfront in dealing with entrepreneurs' anxieties about their marketing strategies while facing rapid algorithm updates and changes. He acknowledges that, yes, we cannot extract our business from social media and online marketing. But there is a possibility of fertilizing each other's businesses by activating smart collaborations. By taking to heart that an expensive advertising campaign is the number one enemy when it comes to budgetary constraints, Gilad shows how two business owners may collaborate to gain massive exposure with minimal investment.

He carefully and thoughtfully shows how you can master your business path to your goals. Instead of chasing the global marketing changing trends. He walks the reader through answering **How should you choose your goals? How should you set your business path? And how could you find opportunities when everyone else sees road blocks?** He provides sensible rules that can keep you on track towards your goals, saving you from costly mistakes and, even better, provides a step-by-step guide to setting fruitful collaborations intended to shorten your road to success.

The second enemy of every entrepreneur is the overabundance of opportunities and inability to stay focused. Small business owners are by definition entrepreneurs, and their radar captures opportunities on a daily basis. Though this sounds nice, in many cases the chase for opportunities distracts them from their destination, often causing them to spin in circles.

In this book Gilad leads the reader to identify and determine their business path and mark it on a map, while providing easy to use measurement tools for choosing between the right and wrong opportunities specific to the reader's business goals.

Finally, enemy number three of any business is working alone. Coming from the Hollywood entertainment industry I can share that studios collaborate in film, record and TV productions - each bringing their own respective strengths to the project. However, when working with small business entrepreneurs I notice that they try to take on the world alone. In this book Gilad brings a new dimension to the table, stating that two businesses do not have to join in a legal contractual partnership, they may simply set a collaboration and join forces in strengthening their respective businesses. He further sets a practical manual, taking the reader hand by hand through the examination of opportunities, while

Introduction

making sure they are staying on course towards achieving their goals.

Finally, Gilad takes the reader through a process of laser-pointing the business and the marketing efforts towards a specific ideal client, while using that specific focus towards initiating collaborations with relevant people and businesses.

> *"I believe very strongly in the value of connecting with other people who share similar business problems and challenges, and with people who have already walked some of the paths you are now walking."*
> – **Kevin Harrington**, known as the $5 Billion entrepreneur

We can hope that more small business entrepreneurs will take Gilad's collaboration message to heart and shortcut their marketing efforts towards success.

He's right. Small business owners are lured to believe that setting a pay per click (PPC) sales funnel is the only legitimate way to expand their reach. Recently, the cost of paid online advertisements has soared. Social media companies are changing their targeting algorithms more frequently than ever before, making Dr. Spencer Johnson's book *Who Moved My Cheese?* or who moved my audience, relevant almost on monthly basis. We meet these business owners almost on a daily basis. They are people that invested all their marketing budget in wrong online campaigns, leaving them at a stalemate. It is for that reason that I see great importance for using different marketing tools at different stages of the business life cycle, and collaborations are a safe marketing shortcut when used appropriately.

But there is an added value to this book. Gilad is declaring his obligation to expanding entrepreneurship know-how to better society by allocating portions of the proceeds to LEAD- *the Youth Leadership Development Organization*, an organization nurturing youth to live a life of social contribution. Identifying that commerce and philanthropy are not polar opposites but rather go hand in hand when done properly. However, the spiritual wellbeing of the reader is not the direct purpose of this book. Gilad Segev does teach us that social contribution may work as a spiritual charger to the exhausted entrepreneur.

Kane Minkus, Bestselling Author, Award Winning Entrepreneur and Founder of Industry Rockstar - #1 Global Business Training Company

FOREWORD

Are you happy with your business standing? Have you accomplished all your goals? Do you manage to dedicate enough quality time to your spouse and children? Are you living a life of abundance you wish to have? Or have you invested a great amount of time and resources in marketing your services or products, only to find that your results are disappointing?

Would you like to discover the single most powerful marketing strategy for low cost leads and major profit?

If you are more interested in reaching success in good faith while increasing your reputation than in arm-wrestling negotiations, you just picked up the right book!

No matter who you are or what your current business situation is, regardless of your age, culture, beliefs or religion, this book is full of insights and will act as a guide in your business life, advising you on the steps to take on your business path to success, and teaching you how to fulfill your goals once you have embarked on your entrepreneurship venture.

From his vast academic learnings, as well as his own years of experiences at the negotiations table, author Gilad Segev has written *Collaborate for Success* so that you can turn your struggle into success, and communicate your interests to other people so that you may together achieve a WIN/WIN conclusion.

Gilad shares with you his personal experiences with small business entrepreneurs, to help you set a practical business path to growth. This guide will help you implement the WIN/WIN negotiation-strategy, whether your business is a one-person business or a multinational organisation.

Get ready to read this amazing guide and create a massive change in your business life and finances.

Raymond Aaron
New York Times Bestselling Author

Chapter 1

Knowing Your Target and Setting Goals

*"If your goals don't scare you and excite you at the same time,
they aren't big enough."*
– Elon Musk

Why Is Goal Setting Crucial?

First things first, do you have a clear life and business goal? Have you written that goal on your screensaver? Are you reading it each day?

I would like to believe all businesses have an identified set goal. But reality is a little different, so first step first.

"A goal is an idea of the future or desired result that a person or a group of people envision, plan and commit to achieve." – Prof. Edwin A. Locke

Let us imagine we are sitting in our nice car. It's a nice summer day, and we have decided to enjoy the opportunity for a family weekend trip. We have packed the food and the family and all are ready for some action. Now what? Where do we go? Do we take the left turn or do we turn right? Or maybe we just need to take the U-turn.

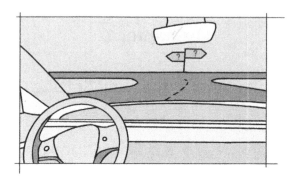

How would that scenario change if we added the following information: You have just left New York City, and your goal is to travel to Niagara Falls. Now your travel plan is much clearer. You will probably set your destination in your GPS app and learn that you need to aim for route 80 and then continue to route 380, and so on.

A Harvard Business study revealed that 83% of the population do not have defined goals, and 14% have a plan in mind but have not bothered to write it down, while only 3% have their goals written down.

The study went on to find that the 14% who have a plan are 10 times more successful than those without goals, while the 3% that invested the effort to write their goals on a piece of paper are 3 times more successful than the 14% with unwritten goals.

My friend, let us recall WHY you have embarked on your current business. What were your initial hopes and goals? Do you still aim toward them? They might have changed through the years because life took you toward a different direction, or maybe because the day-to-day running of the business just keeps you from looking to the future.

I can assume you have invested substantial amounts of time and money into achieving your current abilities, and your clients are attesting that you are very good at what you do. So the starting point for our journey together is that you are an accomplished professional. You know that you are good at what you do; however, for some reason, you have not yet achieved the financial standing and success that you believe you deserve.

I can disclose to you that during my first years of managing my independent business, I had also been pulled away from my dreams. I was buried under a huge pile of mundane tasks. I was focused on survival, doing anything possible to refrain from looking at the bank statement. It took a tragic fall in my business to open my eyes and make me realize the great importance of not only setting a goal but setting the right goal for my business, as well as setting realistic goals for my private, personal life.

Once I had my goals set and polished, my business changed from its reacting mode of activity to an activity-focused business.

The importance and purpose of your goals is to act as a lighthouse. A good set of goals will help you steer the high seas of business progress. Once you set your business and your life goals, your daily routines will feel easier, and your chances of really achieving your goals will be much higher.

You deserve to take your seat with the top 3% whose businesses are thirty times more successful.

How to Set the Right Targets and Goals

When we look at goal setting, we need to examine where we would like to be in our personal lives and in our business lives, in about three to five years' time. There is no need to set the goal for ten years ahead, as too much will change along the way. The goal you set should provide you with a realistic picture of where you would like to be and what you would like to achieve.

As you well know, the day-to-day business life will provide you with your share of challenges. Nothing comes simply because we decided we want it. Therefore, the main criteria in goal setting is to identify something that you are truly passionate about. You are going to relay and recruit that exact passion to overcome the challenges ahead. The greatest mistake people make is to set a financial numeric goal and embark on a business path that seems very smart or a great opportunity, while not being personally passionate about their mission.

Specifying a goal for three years into the future will inevitably cause you to state something that is not so easily achieved. As Robert Brault says, "We are kept from our goal not by obstacles but by **a clear path to a lesser goal.**" This means that it is vital that the goal you set does not seem to be easily achieved at this time. The right goal should not be something that is possible for you to reach within the coming few months. However, it has to be something realistic. For example, if you are not taking part in any political arena, it is unrealistic to state that your goal is to become the prime minister in three years' time.

While identifying your business goal, I also urge you to set your personal or family goal at the same time; reason being that stating, "My goal is to reach a five million dollar income in three years," is not enough. The numerical financial goal will not provide you with enough determination and energy that you will need once hurdles appear.

However, a personal mission and a family goal will provide you with the right energy. Imagine the following situation. You have been working hard marketing your service for several months, and not only did your income not rise, you are actually losing money toward your marketing activities. Do you feel the frustration? I am sure you do.

It is very natural and reasonable. Now let's add the following fact to the equation: You know that your child is about to enter university, or is expected to get married next year. How does that change your motivation? Or maybe your personal goal is to take a six-month vacation and travel around the world. Can you feel the different motivation now?

Therefore, when setting business goals, we need to always attach them to a personal goal since the financial figure itself is not a strong enough motivation tool. The personal goal will provide the WHY needed for your success. *"I need to reach that business goal because I have decided that three years from now, I will take a six-month vacation."* The question you will be asking yourself along the way is, "Why?" Why do I need to work so hard? Why am I banging my head against the wall? The sooner you set your personal goal, the sooner you have a response to that "why."

Another vital consideration that must be addressed while setting your goals is to identify what your passion is. Have you invested enough time in identifying and describing your life passion, in words? Most people do not. When drafting your goal, choose goals that you are passionate about. You will need to revert to that passion each time you experience motivational setbacks.

Connecting your goals to your passions guarantees you an ongoing charge of motivation. And as you have probably heard already, no goal has ever been achieved when a person lacks motivation.

The greater your passion, the easier your road will seem. Make sure you have a strong passion for what you are setting out to do.

Finally, yet important, state the goals by saying "I AM" instead of "I WILL." Imagine yourself as if you have already achieved your goals. Do not say, "In five years' time, I will own 20 apartment units." Rather, "In the summer of 2026, I own 20 apartment units."

Make your goals as specific as you can; draw a vivid picture in your mind, and imagine the smells and your heartbeat when you live your goals. If possible, print and place a picture on the fridge or as a screensaver.

Remember, do not be shy; set high goals and be passionate about them.

> *"We are kept from our goal not by obstacles*
> *but by a clear path to a lesser goal."*
> *– Robert Brault*

Imagine Your Life Once Your Goals Are Achieved

We, as human beings, are basically lazy animals. If we could lie in the sun with a cocktail and a good book, most of us would be very happy. However, you have decided to master your own business, so the cocktail will have to wait. Thus, I recommend you do not forget it.

Knowing Your Target and Setting Goals

Visualizing your goals is very important. Earlier, we noted that we need to place a picture of our goal on the fridge. This is a double-edged sword; if you really wish to push yourself toward your goals, do not hide them. Assuming you do not live alone, and even if you do, write your goals on ten sticky notes and place these around the house. This small act will empower you in two different ways. One is having the mere physical visualization of your goal wherever you go, which will push you toward taking stronger actions aimed at having them materialize. The other is your spouse or children noticing your goals. What will you do in order to not have to tell your child, "I neglected my goals"? Probably a lot... Making your friends and family aware of your goals will fuel your quest to achieve them.

I love the story that Jim Carrey shares on how he applied that piece of advice. In the early 1990s, while he was still an unknown actor, he wrote himself a check for ten million dollars, for "acting services rendered," and he dated it three years ahead. He placed this check in his wallet, and according to him, it made him feel good. He described that it made him imagine this was out there waiting for him. He just hadn't gotten there yet. Then, just before Thanksgiving in 1995, he received a film acting contract for 10 million dollars.

Muhammad Ali, the boxing legend, was always stressing the importance of seeing himself victorious long before the actual fight. And Michael Jordan revealed to us that he always took the last shot in his mind before he ever took one in real life.

The last visualization element that will assist you in your quest is a little X-ray exercise. Please describe to yourself who YOU need to be in order to achieve your goals. You may need to be a sensitive person, spiritual, persistent, gentle or tough. It is vital you are able to dig inside your goals and see what kind of person you need to be when these goals are a reality. It is probable that you are not that person now. It is okay; three years ago, you were a different kind of person too. Once you figure out what kind of person you will be when you achieve your goals, you may start progressing along that path. Make awareness choices to become gentler or more persistent—whatever the case may be.

In a nutshell, visualize your goals happening in the greatest detail possible. This will help you achieve your goals with more ease and quickness.

Prioritize Your Goals

Organizations use the following graphic representation of goal prioritization:

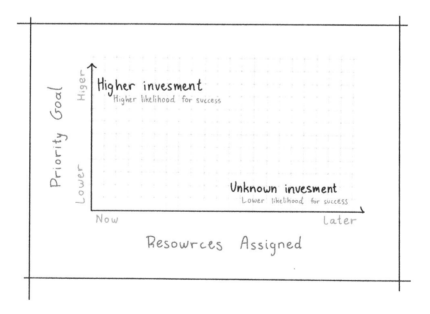

This diagram relates to the correlation between the resources allocated toward achieving each goal, and the implications that allocation has on the likelihood of achieving that goal. The underlying principle is that no organization holds the sufficient funds required to achieve all its goals at the same time.

That does not mean you need to neglect some of your elected goals, but it does stress the need to prioritize them.

A substitutive word for prioritization is "focus." It is about where to assign your attention first; it is not about scoring what is more important for you or your business. Thus, it is about evaluating what is more valuable for you. Avoiding the prioritization stage of goal setting may, in the long run, harm your prospect of achieving your goals. As a demonstration, let us say that you have set only two goals. One goal is to achieve an income level of five million dollars in three years. The other is to be an influential parent. Unfortunately, your resources are limited; like all of us, you have only 24 hours in a day, and 7 days in a week. And you know that achieving your business goal requires you to invest all your time and resources. According to our chart above, this will get you into the "higher likelihood for success." However, what about your second goal? What about making sure you are an influential parent? YouTube CEO, Susan Wojcicki, reveals that she makes it a rule not to check emails between 6 p.m. and 9 p.m. As the mother of five children, she also prioritizes getting home in time for dinner with her family.

Consider the goal prioritization as your compass; it is okay to steer a little to the right or to the left in order to give your attention to more than one singular goal. However, having the main goal at the top of your list will assist you in returning to your desired road for success.

As exampled, your attention and focus will have to be divided between your personal life goals and your business goals. But you may have set several other business goals as well, all of which will have to be prioritized. In any case, it is important to note that combining your personal goals and your business goals will assist in your success. You can set as a goal: "In three years' time, I am making 5 million dollars a year and am traveling with my family for two months each year."

Another dimension for the same prioritization process is the awareness that "life will happen," meaning that we are all aware that things will happen along the way that will demand our attention, our focus and our resources. While we can also expect that, we may choose to change our goals; or our life circumstances may demand that we change our goals, thereby inevitably allowing new goals to emerge. When these occurrences take place, it would be best to go back to our list of goals. At that time, we may be forced or we may wish to remove some older goals from our list.

Having the higher goals identified already, we would be able to save the higher ranking goals and replace one of the other goals as required by our new life or business characteristics.

Here is a little exercise that may assist you in the prioritizing of your goals. If you have listed several goals, all of which are important, set a tournament. Take a piece of paper and organize your goals into pairs. Assess each pair and mark the more important goal. Out of the four goals, you now have two that are marked. Compare these two and mark the winner. Go on until you have one final winner that is your top goal.

Using Your Goals as a Business Tool

We have already compared your goal setting to a compass, guiding your business journey. In this paragraph, I would like us to learn how you can get greater value from your goals.

As we have already learned, your goals should not remain as a vague and illusive idea. Your goals should be written in front of you, providing you with the energy to progress toward achieving them. However, we can do more. We may use our goals as a business tool too.

One of our human "illnesses" is to feel happy with any action we have accomplished. As in this book, we are aiming at growing our businesses, and my intention is not to focus on action but rather to focus on the correct action that will take you and your business to the next level.

Following that clarification, we need to accept that we all try to end our weeks with some pride that we have accomplished some tasks. And as our business life provides us with abundant tasks, we would usually find some way to credit ourselves.

However, now that we have stated our goals, our weekly question should be replaced. Now we should ask ourselves whether we have gotten closer to our goals. The mere asking of this question holds a hidden effect. As we are aware that we would ask ourselves this question, we would stop or reduce our focus on the day-to-day critical goals and focus on what is important to us. So, at the end of the week, our inner report will read, "I am happy that I have solved that critical issue that emerged, and also that I have taken one more step toward my higher goal.

Time your goals. Timing your goals is a great business tool. If my goal were to be an influential parent, I may decide that this requires an investment of three hours per day. With the same attention, I need to identify what time investment is required for the achievement of all my other goals. Note that some future goals may require no attention during this period, and that is okay. I have discovered that marking my goals into weekly time slots in my calendar has led to higher business productivity.

Calendaring your goals may also assist you in your annual plan. Some goals may be more relevant at one specific part of the year. In that case, the annual goal timing becomes important. Your business may be tourist related. That may mean that you experience high growth at certain times of the year—maybe during winter if you are a sky-related business, or during summer if you are sea related.

Marking an achievable goal on the calendar will assist your business activities all year long. Let's get into details. If my business is sea related, and therefore my busy working months are April to September, and I have set my annual income goal at half a million dollars, knowing that my clients pay me $350 per family, I can now assess that I will need to serve 238 families per month (April to September). This has two direct implications. First, I may decide to upgrade my service to serve a smaller number of clients. The second implication is that during wintertime, I may decide to launch a marketing campaign or upgrade my facility to enable me to serve these 240 families per month.

My goals have just become the measurement tool for all my annual and daily business decisions.

Set Your Business Path

Setting your business path is an element rarely spoken about. It is a highly kept secret of business mentors.

So, what is a business path? The business path is the way you design for yourself and your business in order to reach your goals. Let me give you an example. Let us say you are a sport coach, and you have decided that your goal to be reached in three years' time is to "be considered the number one coach in the state." Currently, you are coaching youth in a local gym.

Knowing your goal, we can identify at least two alternative meanings for the same goal, while each meaning will lead you through a very different path. With option one, you may decide that the meaning of being the best coach in your state is to lead three of your athletes to the national level, international ranking or even the Olympics.

That interpretation of your goal—being considered the number one coach in the state—will entail the following path. You would need to focus on identifying the most prominent youth. You would need to coach these young athletes day by day, week by week. You would need to assist them in receiving sponsorships. By the way, that is your income. Your plan would have to include a wide enough group of athletes at different ages, from which you would identify the leaders so as to get them one by one toward their goals and achievements, whereby your goal shall be achieved.

With option two, you may decide that your goal of "being considered the number one coach in the state" will mean that you shall coach the largest number of athletes in your state. This interpretation will lead you via a very different business path. You may start with opening your own local gym, and recruiting coaches and groups of athletes wishing to improve their skills. In the second phase, you may develop your own coaching methods. So while your athletes are getting better and better, your method reputation is exceeding. The following phase may be to expand your reach outside your neighborhood or town, open branches or franchise your method. Growing via that path continuously may also place you at the top of the pyramid. Choosing this interpretation, you would be the one coaching the largest number of athletes, which would mean that you have concurred your goal of "being considered the number one coach in the state."

Here we see two very different ways for reaching the exact same goal. This was an example, and the same would apply to any type of business and for any goal you have set.

Setting your business path is a vital element in making sure you conquer your goals.

While meeting with my mentees, we not only search for several paths for each goal, but we also dig into the psychological needs and wishes of each business owner, as different business paths also entail a different spiritual or emotional identity of the person setting the goals.

If we go back to our coach, we can now note that walking the first path would be suitable for a person that is highly motivated for achieving international recognition. He would also have to be a person that has the personal ability to push his athletes every day toward higher results. He is a person that is good at focusing on a small number of students, one on one.

On the other hand, if our coach chooses the second path, most of his time would not be spent with his athletes. Yes, he has to be a good coach, but he would also have to own some higher level of group teaching abilities. His new teaching techniques would have to be so unique that athletes from other towns would wish to be practicing with him. Once that phase is achieved, most of his activity would turn to growing the gym chain business, managing or franchising other instructors in other locations, while dedicating his life to growing his chain of gyms. Now he is a businessperson.

As you can now see, setting your goal is the first step. It may be the most important stage; however, it is not enough. Getting into details, searching your soul and writing your path is a vital part of any successful goal setting.

Track Your Progress

If you have followed the above stages, and drafted along your remarks and comments, you are now much closer to your happiness, for the simple reason that you know where you would be happy to be in three or five years' time.

Or is it so? Let us return and observe what is happening at the larger international organizations. As you probably know, the headquarters have stated the organization's goals, and from that moment onwards. Each division and each team would conduct periodical meetings to report what steps have been taken. They will also report the setbacks encountered. The underlying practice behind those periodical board meetings is the fact that the HQ goals came down to the divisions accompanied by a numerical description of the achievements required. Therefore, each team is able to report whether they managed to achieve their targets or not.

The same practice must take place at your business. It does not matter if you are a multibillion dollar business or a single, self-employed professional. Your goal must be described by a figure. There is no sense in setting a goal if you will never know whether you have achieved it or not. Going back to our coach, he would obviously need to know whether the current largest chain of gyms, relevant to his field of sport, owns five branches or fifty branches. If you wish to determine the level of success that you achieve, you must be able to measure your progress.

Measuring your progress will act as a great motivator. Good progress will push you forward with greater energy. The sooner you identify that you are not making sufficient progress, you will be able to pause and identify the changes needed so that you get back on track.

Measuring your progress is the lifeline that would eventually lead you to success in achieving your goals. Therefore, attached to each goal, we need to now set a measurable target. For example, rather than saying "I want to lose weight," you would need to write, "I want to lose 15pounds." Rather than saying "I want to be considered as the best coach in the state," our friend would now have to say, "My goal is to get two of my athletes to international competitions, or to own 25 gyms."

The following step is to measure your progress. Not all measuring methods are relevant to all businesses, so your task is to choose your relevant or preferred measuring method.

By far the easiest way is simply by having a quantified goal. For example, my goal is to make such and such an amount of dollars, to have a such and such number of clients, or to lose a such and such amount of weight. Following the numbers would show you exactly how fast you are progressing toward your goal.

A second tracking method is by setting a time per task. Earlier, you identified your business path. Not all stages may be quantified by dollar amounts. In the following chapter, we will look into setting your smaller tasks along that path. For now, it is sufficient to say that scheduling your tasks is also a good way of tracking your progress. You may state that you need to accomplish a specific task by next Monday. Come Monday morning, if that task was not achieved, then you have your answer.

Once you have identified the most suitable tracking method for your business and goals, it is vital to keep records and checklists. Your records are one of your most important tools for success. They serve you well, no matter what happened in reality, whether you succeeded in accomplishing your task or not. If you did not succeed, the records will reveal what went wrong, saving you from paying for the same mistake all over again. Thus, more important are your success records. Once an action you took has progressed you toward your goal, you would probably wish to amplify it all over again so that your progress would be faster. People often overlook their accomplishments and spend time on studying their failures. When working with my mentees, I direct them to act exactly the opposite. We can usually easily understand what went wrong; however, if we deeply analyze what went right, jumping on the fast train forward becomes much easier.

Note that not all goals are suitable for numeric measurements. If that is the case, you would need to set your own personal scale. One common medical example is the pain scale. Obviously, each person feels pain differently; however, medical research needs to present if a specific treatment is reducing pain or is painful. The scale designed is subjective. Each person would describe his level of pain from 1 to 10. While we are aware that level 5 for one person may be very different from level 5 for the other, this non-objective scale works just fine as a statistical tool. Going back to your goals, you may have set a confidence goal, wishing to achieve better confidence. For that, you would need to create your own confidence gauge so that you may measure your progress.

Once your progress tracking system is in place, a weekly or monthly observation would provide you with the best GPS of your progress toward your set goals.

Chapter 2

Set Your Missions and Objectives

"There are different ways to do innovation. You can plant a lot of seeds, not be committed to any particular one of them, but just see what grows. And this really isn't how we've approached this. We go mission-first, then focus on the pieces we need and go deep on them and be committed to them."
— Mark Zuckerberg

What Are Objectives?

What is the difference between a goal, an objective and a task?

How do they relate and work together?

The goal represents the reason why we set out on a particular path. It indicates what we want to achieve at the end, and is therefore the source of motivation for taking action.

The goal is the criterion for selecting relevant tasks, meeting schedules, allocating resources, etc.

Objectives are actually like intermediate goals. They are the indicators that we are moving in the right direction, toward the desired goal. They are necessary as milestones, similar to the steps in the ladder. Therefore, they need to be clear, measurable and defined by a pre-determined schedule.

To illustrate that, let us go back to our coach, whose goal is to own the largest gym chain in the state. His first set objective may be to expand and open a further 2 to 3 gyms in his own city, within six months; while the second stage objective could be to open one gym per town in five other towns within a year, and so on.

Just like your goals, each objective should be accompanied by clear, measurable criteria. That will allow the examination of the achievement of said objective, in full or in part.

However, as you have noticed, the objectives to be reached entail a complicated process. It is not so obvious to triple the size of your business in three months, or to open eight new branches within a year. Basically, the objectives are mini goals that we place along our business path toward our main goals.

In order to achieve our objectives, we need to assign and identify the smaller steps that should be taken. These smaller steps are our missions, while the even smaller marks to be accomplished are the tasks. The tasks are the day-to-day or weekly activities you would set in your calendar. A task should be small and simple, feasible and realistic. Performing a series of tasks successfully will ensure you complete your mission, just as each mile consists of some 2,250 walking steps.

Working with a team would require the team leader to assign the clear tasks to each team member, in a way that makes it clear who is doing what, when, by what means and so on.

Set Your Missions and Objections

In this chapter, I would like to focus on the importance of setting the right missions. As the missions are the stepping stones that may allow us flexibility in the business, we may need to assess once reality takes place. Note that I do not call the events that will take you off your path, surprises, as we are not really surprised by them. We know that our plan will not materialize "as is." We know some event will happen along the way, which will take us off course, while part of our business plan toward our goal will have to allow some flexibility so that these events will not take us completely off the map.

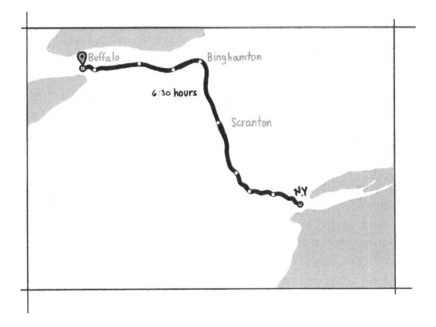

As a short summary of our discussion until now, let us go back to our weekend family trip from NYC to Niagara Falls. Our goal at the end of the road is to reach the cliffs of the falls. The time frame we set is six and a half hours. Our objective may be to drive along the fastest route, while our first mission would be passing through

Scranton, our second mission passing through Binghamton, and the third reaching Buffalo.

Explore Your Chosen Business Path

Preparing your business path is almost as complex an operation as a military operation. But note that planning your business path involves great satisfaction, which is felt the moment you are able to visualize yourself achieving your goals.

The more effort invested in planning the business path, the easier it would be to see goals materializing. A top secret for designing the best path would be to get a mentor. A business mentor is a person that has already achieved your exact goals and is therefore able to provide great assistance in knowing the best path to follow. The mentor's experience should be used for saving you from choosing the difficult path, while pointing out the best shortcuts available toward achieving your goals.

Once you have identified your complete business path, it is recommended you dig into the details. If we yet again return to our coach and examine his first objective of owning three gyms in his hometown, we now need to make sure we understand and visualize the steps we need to take in order to achieve that objective. Our first mission may be to increase the number of athletes practicing in our gym, to a hundred. Alternatively, we may choose to coach ten different groups of athletes at our first gym before we expand to the next, while getting our mentor's advice may lead us to change the order of things, and we may set the first mission at opening the second gym regardless of how many athletes practice at our current gym.

Set Your Missions and Objections

Following the same logic, you should now map your own business path. Explore each objective along the way, and set the intermediate missions so that the objectives do not seem intimidating. At this stage, there is no need to specify your weekly tasks. But you are required to understand WHY you have chosen that business path. What is the purpose of each large milestone or objective along the way, and why have you set the smaller milestones, the missions, as you have done.

The purpose of this exercise is to achieve happiness. The happiness will come once you feel that the business path you have set is a realistic one, and once you are able to visualize your business progressing and accomplishing, mission by mission, along the way.

It is reasonable to feel that some of your future objectives are daunting; as from your current position, they are really too complicated to be achieved. You may not even hold the sufficient know-how and understanding of how to approach these tasks. It is okay; you do not have to know everything now. However, visualizing the complete road ahead should make you smile.

Remember, Rome was not built in a day. That is why your goal is three years ahead; you should not feel that it is easily approachable. By the way, if your goal seems approachable, I urge you to consider increasing your goals.

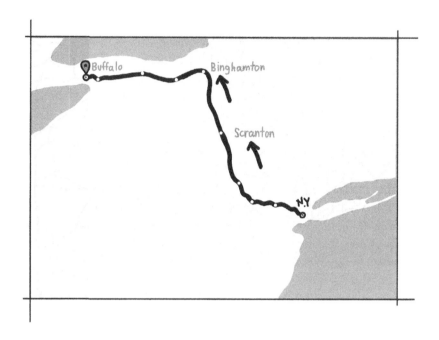

By plotting our complete business path toward our goals, we in effect take a pincer movement. We keep one eye on our goals, while the other eye observes our progress toward our nearest mission.

By now, we have completely shifted our business position. In the first pages of this book, we imagined being in our car, embarking on a weekend family trip, but we were not sure what turn we should take. Now you are sitting in the driver's seat, possessing full control over your future. You now know where you are heading, what your goal is, and you have chosen exactly which of the alternative roads would lead you toward your goals.

In the upcoming paragraph, we will discover how to react when our plans do not come true.

Persist Over the Correct Missions

As we are all aware, not all plans materialize exactly as we earlier envisaged them on the drawing board. We have left NYC behind and are driving due west along route 80. We have specified that our first mission shall be to pass through Scranton. At the moment, we have completed several tasks, and we are some 45 miles away from our first mission. All seems to be going according to plan. But then our GPS app provides us with an update: The road ahead is periodically blocked due to construction work.

The direct implication is that our trip just got longer by some ninety minutes. You are facing a dilemma: Your business plan dictates you complete each mission if you are to achieve your goals. You do not intend to let the changing circumstances steer you away from your mission; you are most passionate about your goals, and you are energized to tackle any obstacle.

As we already mentioned earlier, changing circumstances are no big surprise. Thus, a global pandemic may take the world by surprise, but you as an entrepreneur are aware that some surprises will occur along the way, meaning you are not surprised. Nevertheless, you do need to consider these changing circumstances.

Let me now reveal an important rule that should act as your guideline. The mission is important as long as it leads you toward your goal. In reverse, the mission stops being important if circumstances have changed, and by completing the mission, you will not get closer to your goal. You may even get farther from your goal.

In setting our missions, we identified a few important milestones. Accomplishing each milestone would get us closer to our goals, step by step. We later chartered a detailed strategy for accomplishing each mission. These missions are important to us and are not so easy to accomplish.

However, something happened: circumstances changed. The change does not have to be negative; it could just as well be a very positive one. As opposed to that roadblock, it is also possible to imagine that some friend called us, disclosing that he is taking his helicopter toward our exact destination, and we can join him and save a few hours of driving. Imaginary? Maybe, but you get the point. Anything can happen. In both scenarios, we would be facing the same dilemma. In which instance do we choose to refrain from achieving our mission?

These are the times when you use the above rule as your guideline. If persisting over this mission would still get you closer to your goals, then that is what you must do. There are no shortcuts on the road to success. However, if the persistence over solving this obstacle will push your goals further away, then this is the time to look for an alternative route, be it a short bypass or maybe even substantially changing your over-all game plan.

As per our expected roadblock on our way to Niagara Falls, we may discover that one option is to persist with our pre-set plan and suffer a delay of ninety minutes. Alternatively, our GPS app may disclose that we can choose an alternative route; a route that may be 10 miles longer but would actually get us to our destination much faster. In that example, it is somewhat clear that you would choose the open route and refrain from persisting on accomplishing that specific mission.

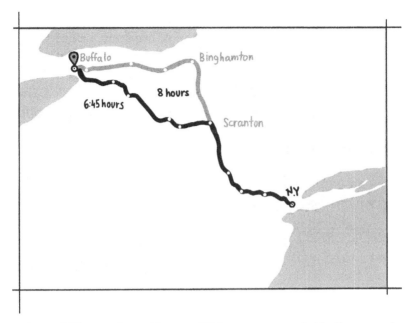

In real life, we do not have a GPS app or a crystal ball, so we do not have definite foresight of what will happen once we deviate from our plan. Nevertheless, the same rule would apply: The mission is important only as long as it brings you closer toward achieving your set goals.

Opportunities and Hurdles

We have talked about road/business bumps and hurdles, but our business life is not that grim. From time to time, we encounter opportunities. According to the *Cambridge Dictionary*, an opportunity is an occasion or situation that makes it possible to do something that you want to do or have to do.

Do you remember that we mentioned that on your way to Niagara Falls, a helicopter landed and offered you a ride? That is an opportunity to save traveling time. Though it sounds great, your weekend plan may have included other activities. Therefore, you should consider whether leaving your car behind would serve your weekend plans, or would it just get you to your first destination faster, while from that stage onward, you would be unable to proceed and accomplish your future missions?

As an entrepreneur, you are aware that opportunities exist everywhere and all the time. I am certain that you can think of at least one example where you were thinking of some idea, and suddenly, within a few days, some friend called you, or you had seen a news interview, revealing some opportunity relating exactly to your thoughts.

At this stage, as we have identified and chosen our business path, we have embarked on accomplishing our missions toward our goals. At this stage, we have a new business obligation. We are obligated to examine each opportunity with our goal in mind. Please contemplate the following: an opportunity that would require half of your time for the coming months and would reward you with double your current income during that period. Is it a good opportunity or a bad one? Would your response be different if it implies that your goal has to be postponed for another year?

Let us return to our coach and examine a real business-life opportunity. You are coaching as an employee at the local gym. You have set your goal that in five years' time, you would become the number one coach in the state. You have also chosen your business path. It states that you will be considered the best coach because two of your athletes have passed the Olympic qualifications. Five months into your business journey, you get a call. On the other end is an old-time friend, and after a short talk, he comes up with an offer. He tells you that together with some investors, he is now the proud owner of the largest gym in the capital. He discloses to you that he must now get the best manager for that gym, and if you agree, the position is yours. You learn that the salary would be great, and he will take care of all your moving expenses, plus you will get a company car. In relation to their future plans, you hear that they plan to expand, and the manager of the main branch would be expected to join the HQ when the time comes. All in all, it's a great opportunity.

However, what about the Olympics? What about your goals? Obviously, you will not be able to accomplish both goals simultaneously. Thus, no one can make your choices for you.

A human being is not a machine; you have more than one set of considerations. When contemplating your options, you would probably also consider what would be best for your spouse and your children. It is true that you are focused on your goals, but these are your goals. You are free to decide that circumstances have provided you with such an opportunity that you will now reorganize your personal life and your business life accordingly. It is okay; this is your life, and you are free to change your goals.

However, the main lesson here is that such a decision is a critical decision, to be made after hard consideration and with total understanding of the new path ahead. If you make the decision to set new goals, be advised that you do need to set a new business path that will lead you toward your new goals.

Are All Opportunities Good?

We know setbacks are bad, but are all opportunities good? Earlier, we noted that there is no simple answer. From my experience with many businesses, I know that this is a crucial issue. Many business owners are, by definition, entrepreneurs. The excitement of new opportunities fuels our imagination. We hear of an opportunity, and we are drawn toward exploring it, like a mosquito to the light.

At this stage, I would like you to climb into your business driver's seat. You may manage a one-person show; you are the only person in your business, and you are in charge of everything. You have to take your wagon driver's seat. Your horse sees the mission ahead and is heading forward. Now you spot an opportunity to the right—do you turn right? Many business owners would. They would turn right to explore that opportunity. It is in our nature. In a week's time, a new opportunity would arise to the right, again. What do we do? The same—we turn right. Before too long, your business wagon is going in circles. And your goals... what goals?!

Researching my mentees, I noticed that there are set behaviors for young business owners, and other behaviors taken by more experienced persons. However, the successful business owners do something else.

In many cases, young business owners would act just like the above example and go in circles. I would usually meet them after two years, and they would be exhausted. They would have invested all their resources into exploring many opportunities. But their wagon is almost at the same spot where they started. More mature people usually utilize their life experience and are not tempted by all opportunities. They would accept some and reject some. They would invest fewer resources at each emerging opportunity. However, they still view themselves as entrepreneurs; thus, they cannot ignore all opportunities. The result is that their business wagon travels in a zigzag pattern. It does progress toward the goal, but it loses a lot of time and resources along the way.

Experienced business owners practice the third practice, which is the most important for you to embrace at this stage. They would have their own personal system for examining opportunities. For them, each opportunity would be placed into that well-oiled system. For me, that opportunity assessment takes a week. I would explore the opportunity through a specific mode, and I would consider the opportunity against other ideas and products I have met in the past, while also placing the opportunity in vision of market forecasts. After a week, I usually have a better feeling if there is a need to start investing resources in exploring that opportunity. You would need to develop your own crystal ball—some opportunity examination method that would work well for you.

The experienced business owners would not suffer from the zigzag pattern, but their wagons would not go in a direct straight line toward the goals—that never happens. They would move aside from the straight line, with small movements to the right and left, but they would never lose sight of the goal ahead.

Once you master the collaboration technique, many opportunities will emerge each week. The ability to assess them and direct your attention only toward the right opportunities is an important skill you will have to master.

Collaborations as the Main Tool for Success

Now we are ready to discover the secret that all social media marketers are missing: how to increase sales with ease by using the correct collaborations technique.

The secret we are going to reveal in this book will revolutionize your thoughts, and later on, your income and business position, to such an extent that you will never look back.

Our journey together had to start with the deep understanding of goal setting and the importance of setting your correct business missions and milestones along your path. As we embark on collecting opportunities, it is also vital to note that not all opportunities should be embraced. Once we have accomplished these objectives, we are now ready to discover the great collaboration set of tools.

Like any tool, this tool is here to serve a purpose. It should be used at the right time, while other business tools, like setting a marketing plan or finance-related working system, should not be neglected.

Reiterating the obvious, as funny as it may be, seems required during these times. We need to remind ourselves that human interaction creates business at least as well as the internet and social media; and may I say, much more.

Just like you, I was also disappointed by the continuous flow of online marketers trying to convince me that the only way to reach clients and sales is by paying or investing in PPC (pay per click) at the various social media platforms or online search engines. The purpose of this book is to show you that there are other ways, at lower costs and higher success rates. That is, through correct collaborations.

I hope you are now wondering why I named it "correct" collaborations. This is simply to distinguish that not all collaboration opportunities are the same—and may I add, not the same for your specific business. We will reveal which collaborations are good for you, and which may just drain your time and attention. Each business should search for different collaborations that will be complementary to its activity. Our goal is to utilize these collaborations for increasing our sales and revenue continuously.

What Is a Collaboration?

One last pause before we jump into the deep negotiation techniques. Let us set our board game. You are probably expecting this book to assist in your quest for collaborating with other people or businesses for marketing benefits, and you are right. However, before you approach someone and set your joint venture, I would like to distinguish a few legal terms, using the *Cambridge Dictionary*:

Partnership: A company that is owned by two or more people.

Joint Venture (JV): A business or business activity that two or more people or companies work on together.

Collaboration: The situation of two or more people working together to create or achieve the same thing.

In general terms, a partnership is a legal entity backed by detailed agreements between two or more parties. An example could be two movie studios that have partnered for the production of a new film. Each will continue their normal business activity while they set a partnership for that specific production. A JV would also be supported by detailed legal agreements; thus, no new company is being registered. The parties to the JV would usually be highly invested into their JV. We would see many of these at the high-tech business arena.

This book is not intended for the management personnel of such companies, though sales teams and marketing managers may find it very useful.

Entrepreneurs, self-employed people and small businesses look for something else. We look for collaborations. A collaboration is a way for a person to work with another while maintaining his independence. The parties will have to agree what activities are required to be taken by each of them, and what the reward is. But they do not require complicated legal agreements. In fact, the collaboration will last as long as both parties are happy with the results they are receiving out of it. It could last for years or be rejected very shortly after the handshake.

The backbone of the collaboration would be the ongoing benefit each of them receive. The benefits could be financial but could also be anything that assists each of them in getting closer to achieving their goals. As such, the benefit each receives does not have to be the same.

A good collaboration should get you a flow of incoming clients on a regular basis. Depending on the collaboration and your field of business, nevertheless, it's a powerful marketing tool. A correct collaboration would have me connect with a person or a company that is *able and willing* to direct the *right clients* toward my business.

Chapter 3

Set a Mutual Agreed Baseline

"I will talk about two sets of things. One is how productivity and collaboration are reinventing the nature of work, and how this will be very important for the global economy...."
– Satya Nadella

What Is a Good Collaboration for You?

Is it a collaboration if I agree with a friend that I will send clients in his direction, and vice versa, he will recommend my services or products to his friends?

What will your opinion be if we add that you also agree to pass a small payment to your friend for every client that actually buys your service (a referral fee)? Would you consider that as a collaboration?

I would say both are nice to have, but I would not consider either as a good collaboration. I invite you to revert back to your life and business experience. How many times did you ask people to refer clients to your business? How many clients did eventually appear at your doorstep as a result of each of these friend referrals? I am sure some clients did approach your business due to these referrals, as this is the best referral system that exists. It is called word-of-mouth referrals, and we would utilize it later. However, at this stage, I urge you to count how many clients came from EACH of these friends. The response would be, not too many.

This means that expecting real income generation from the referrals of a single person is not realistic. It is not stable enough that you can consider it as a main business tool in your arsenal, though I do recommend you ask your friends to refer people toward your products.

I would like to suggest that:

- A good collaboration is one that provides your business with a stable ongoing flow of clients.
- A good collaboration will save you marketing time, money and efforts.
- A good collaboration will save you client service time.
- A good collaboration will shorten your sales process.

Let us return to our above agreement with our friend, and get it down to reality. We had met Dan in a networking meeting, and we had a very friendly conversation. Our coffee meeting concluded by coming to an understanding that we would both benefit if we send each other clients. Two days later, I received a call from a potential new client. During the call, I learned that he had been referred to me by Dan. That was great news, and it reminded me that I should also try to reciprocate by pointing someone toward Dan as well. But why did that not turn into a flow of clients? What is missing here? How would the result change if I had agreed with Dan that for each referred client, we would pass $75 between us as a referral fee? How would my business look then?

Set a Mutual Agreed Baseline

In truth, my business would look almost the same. Yes, it is true that Dan would be happy to receive my referral fee, and this would motivate him to send another client toward my business. However, that referral fee would not be so substantial for Dan's business. He would be happy to receive these small bonuses from time to time, but he would not invest any special effort every day just for that small amount. Therefore, we can't rely on such a friendly referral system as one of our business modules.

If we stated that a good collaboration is the best marketing tool you should manage in your arsenal, then obviously it means something else.

The purpose of this book is to take you step by step through the technique that would result in a continuous flow of clients. Earlier, you wrote down your goals and even stated your business path and missions. For now, let us say that one of your missions states you need to increase the number of paying clients entering your business. So one of your tasks would state you need to find some good people that will refer these potential clients.

Once you embrace this set of skills, opportunities will fall into your lap every day. May I ask, would you consider your competitors as people that you might collaborate with?

At the outskirts of our city, there is an industrial area where many small furniture shops are located. Some are family businesses and some are branches of some larger chains. As such, people know that when they are looking to renovate, they should include that area when they are shopping around. But then, some ten years ago, a larger international furniture chain announced that they were going to open a shop in that area, and the shop floor was to be 6.2 acres (25,000 sq. meters). So you can imagine the local businesses were protesting. The competition was going to be unfair. Eventually, that shop was opened, and what happened? All other furniture businesses in that area are flourishing; the reason being that the direct competition was not the only outcome.

Further outcomes included the construction of a huge parking lot, which solved a long-time logistic nightmare for clients coming to that area. The extensive marketing made by the new shop, caused people to travel to that specific industrial area from cities farther away, substantially increasing the number of clients entering the shopping area. People like to do some window shopping and, thus, many would enter the older shops, increasing their sales volume. Even the greatest shop does not offer everything to everyone, so clients started visiting the neighboring shops, searching for solutions to their specific needs. The lesson we need to take from that story is that in the right setting, we need not rule out setting a good collaboration with a competitor.

Imagine a client going to that new large furniture shop with a list of wishes for a sofa, a shelf and so on. Exiting the shop with only part of his list fulfilled, he would leave his car in that same parking space and walk to the neighboring shops, searching for the remaining items on his list. He would purchase the high-end sofa at one shop, and he could find the simple library shelf at the second, while saving an hour of commuting and searching for a new parking spot.

This is the principle for a good collaboration: two competing businesses realizing that together they can serve their clients better. Note that although this could be achieved, a much easier and much recommended collaboration would be to unite with a business that is not your competitor. Rather, a successful collaboration would come from uniting with a business that is fulfilling your clients' needs but is not competing with you in the same niche. The aim is to create a situation that leads the client to feeling that 1+ 1 = 3. When the client has that feeling, you have set the correct collaboration.

So, what is a good collaboration for you? What do you want to achieve out of that collaboration, other than money? What is the result you would like to achieve, which would get you closer to your goals? That would help you accomplish the missions you have set.

The best collaboration you can set is one that solves one of your main business problems. Consider all elements of your business, not only the sales. Identify what hurdles and problems you are facing, and see how collaborating with the right business would solve that specific difficulty.

Once you know your collaboration goal, you are ready for the next step.

What Is an Agreed Baseline?

Our main goal in planning a correct collaboration is to get the client to feel that he was upgraded. The client has to come out on top. Once that is achieved, both of the collaborators can report a WIN. This is a totally different situation from one business passing some referral fee to the other. I hope you start to feel the excitement.

Earlier, we discussed the mutual referral relationship. While agreeing to mutually refer clients, we can assess that one of us would be more active in referring clients to the other. So if you sent four clients to me, but I only sent one potential client to you, it is clear that pretty soon you would stop bothering to send me clients. That scenario would not change much if some commission passed between us, as the payment would usually be a small amount per client and not a real motivation provider, which means that this is not a situation whereby both parties can register a WIN.

However, if the client can report a big WIN, then altogether something else has occurred. This is a good indicator that both of the collaborators can register a substantial WIN, as well as the client.

That is the baseline when planning a correct collaboration.

Debby is a mom instructor; her niche is teaching young mothers how to get their babies to fall asleep faster and be calmer. Yael teaches infant movement classes for young mothers with toddlers. As such, both ladies do not meet; each are investing in their own marketing efforts, and each are trying to stand out from their competitors. Now I would like you to join me and get the bird's-eye perspective. Both work with similar clients—not identical but similar. Debby's clients are mothers of newborn babies that are having a hard time going to sleep, while Yael is working with toddlers a few months old and up to six years old.

The first time I met them, they could not see how they could collaborate. By the way, the mere fact that most businesses do not realize the potential, makes it easier for you to grab the opportunity and grow your business.

I had to reveal to them that their collaboration could lead them toward 1+1=3. That same mother whose baby is experiencing difficulties going to sleep, has another child at home, who is three years old; while the other mother that goes to the infant movement class with her four year old, is now pregnant and will soon have a newborn who might experience difficulties going to sleep.

When climbing up to the bird's-eye view, we can discover that although Debby and Yael are working in different market niches, their different clients may just be the same person. Both are investing in marketing, branding and building client relationships, all for a relatively short period of time, until the babies/children get older and are no longer in need of their services. Furthermore, after a relatively short time, both disconnect from the old clients and start approaching potential new clients all over again.

The alternative could come in the following form. The sleep instructor visits one of the infant movement classes and teaches the mothers some nice ideas. She immediately gains exposure, publicity and, hopefully, some new clients. But she also receives something much greater, and for no cost: She receives TRUST.

The class participants already trust their teacher, so that same trust passes immediately to the visiting sleep instructor. The benefit of gaining free trust of your potential clients is priceless, and it is a big WIN for Debby. On top of that, she gets a chance to talk directly to her potential clients, to look them in the eyes and respond to their questions. Some would immediately become clients as they have another baby at home, and some would share their experience with a friend who is struggling with putting her baby to bed. They would recommend the guest, just because she was a guest of the teacher they trust. No marketing costs, no sales efforts, direct access to the ideal customers—all by riding on the teacher's reputation with her clients. Obviously, Yael, the infant movement instructor, will visit Debby's groups too, and gain same benefits.

The baseline is the answer for the following questions:

- What is my goal?
- What is the mission I am focused on achieving now?
- What interests do I want to get solved by this collaboration?
- According to my assessment, what may be the interests of the other person?
- Am I willing and able to provide a solution to their needs?

Prepare Your Presentation of the Baseline

We have seen in the previous example that Debby did pass out Yael's business cards, but that was not the conversation. The conversation was based on identifying a situation where an action taken by one collaborator would lead the other collaborator to make a profit—a profit in financial terms, marketing terms and in gaining clients' trust at no cost.

Our goal in setting a good, long-lasting collaboration, is to identify the contribution we would like to receive out of that collaboration. Yes, the easy response is "income." But there may be a smarter response. True, per the above example, when visiting the other professional's class, you may get some direct orders, which could materialize into a nice flow if you set a few similar

Set a Mutual Agreed Baseline

collaborations and, once a week, visit a different class. However, there is much more to gain. Let's talk about the trust you gain. The trust you gain will assist in building your brand. The class participants that are not your potential clients, may pass your information on to their friends and family as they now trust you. Remember that there is another hidden benefit you have in front of these non-clients: They do not view your competitor's advertisements, and they are not interested in your competitor's service, and this is good news.

Just because you have now gained the trust of that mother who is participating in the infant-movement class, she is not your potential client, so she has no barriers in hearing your message. However, her sister just gave birth to a loud baby. Her sister is your potential client; as such, she is bombarded by all relevant advertisements, and her brain does the obvious and blocks them all out. However, at night, when she talks to her sister, no barriers are up. Her sister, who had just met you this morning, trusts that you are very good because she trusts her class instructor, who is now collaborating with you. She will share that feeling with her sister; no spam barriers are up, and you just won a new client.

That is the meaning of gaining free client trust.

Once you decide what your WIN is, out of the collaboration you are about to set, consider who is the best partner that can and will be glad to provide that WIN for you.

Make a list of all professions and businesses that are relevant to enabling your WIN.

See if your contact list, or your friends' contact lists, include some of these people. At the same time, start contemplating what benefits and advantages you may provide these people or businesses.

Note that they may not have read this book, so you can either give them this book or you would need to set the agreed baseline for the discussion yourself. We will tackle that in the next chapter. For now, you just need to be aware that the baseline does consist of two main elements. One is your understanding and decision on what you wish to gain from each collaboration; the other is making an educated guess on what your partner may wish to gain. And see that you yourself are happy to provide the other person with the benefits you think he may ask for.

This is an important element. If you do not believe that person is a good professional, then providing him with your clients' trust may backfire in your business, and your clients will lose trust in you once they are not happy with his service. So, do your homework before proceeding.

Your presentation of your interests and, later, at the right time, providing your responses to the other person's interests, is the starting point of a good collaboration.

Assess Timing Probability

Part of our homework, before the collaboration-setting meeting, is figuring out, to the best of our knowledge, whether this collaboration would do us good. Once we are happy with the prospect, the whole process has higher chances for success. The need for preparation is also used as your safety belt. As your energy is not limitless, you have an interest to maximize the results of each presentation. When planning for a fundraising road show, there is an understanding that most of the people you are going to meet will reject the opportunity, but you need only one. Therefore, a start-up will invest any resources available in achieving that goal.

For you, this is not the case; you are planning on using collaboration as one of your business tools. If all goes well, you will set several collaborations on your business path, aiming at accomplishing different missions along the way. So, you need a high success rate at setting these collaborations. As such, let's see how we can increase your closing rate at these meetings, through some preparation techniques.

Above, we set a few questions you need to ask yourself. Now let us observe and learn about our potential collaborator. Obviously, it takes two to tango, and right now we are standing alone. But approaching just any person on the street will probably lead to an awkward dance. Therefore, we need to assess our success probabilities even before investing more resources.

Let us return to our two instructors. I am working with mothers of babies; and the other, the infant-movement instructor, is working with mothers of toddlers up to the age of six. When contemplating the collaboration, as we exampled earlier, noting that I am new to that town, my main interest is to strengthen my brand in the same geographical territory in which the other is working already. My second interest is to test the price levels these leads will pay for my service, as selling cheap is not a smart trick. My third interest is to get my first two groups open as soon as possible.

Only in light of my interests, I can assess the chances of succeeding with that person, as my interests will determine what information I need to collect, even at this early stage. Because I have decided that one of my interests is strengthening my brand, I must make sure the other business brand is a highly esteemed brand. If their products are sold at market bottom prices, then there is no trust there for me to win. I would like to learn that the other instructor's clients are coming to her repeatedly with every newborn baby, and that they are willing to pay high tuition fees, as she is so good. This means that if she says to her trusting clients that I am good at what I do, then I can assess that my brand has already climbed to higher ground.

You would need to develop some examination methods to assure that most of your interests could be fulfilled by collaborating with that business.

A further element that will always have to be satisfied is the internal and external timing. Both have to be in favor of this collaboration, for it to succeed.

The external timing is events and market trends that are affecting your potential collaborator. Take the COVID pandemic that is upon us (as of early 2020). The lockdowns may have caused the other business to suffer, whereby they are now just looking to survive. They are practically not working, and there is definitely not much chance that your brand can benefit from making any plans with them at this stage. On the other hand, they may have made the needed adjustments, such as teaching their classes via live online platforms. In fact, their service may be in huge demand because their clients are losing their minds during the lockdown. Her clients now perceive her as their savior, and they will do anything she says; and by recommending you, your brand will receive an immediate boost—same external timing, two very different results.

I assume if you had to choose between the two businesses, you would definitely approach the second.

Another example, during the pandemic, may be setting your mission at a collaboration with a well-known celebrity. In usual times, this may be a very expensive task, one that you cannot afford. However, in lockdown, even celebrities need to remain visible to their audience, and maybe collaborating with your service is just what they need.

The internal timing refers to the business life stage. This is a more elusive criteria, but if you get a red indicator, you may just save yourself a lot of time. As you would like to provide the other business with an important WIN, you would like to assess that you approach them at the right time. Please be aware that at this stage, you are only making educated guesses. In our instructor's collaboration example, we may conclude that the other person will only enjoy presenting their service to our clientele as long as we are serving the same size of audience or greater. If we are new in town, we may need to offer some other benefit. That does not mean that you can only set collaborations with businesses your size.

Several years ago, I was involved in setting the collaboration between one of the larger banks and a very small business. The small business only had six employees. You may ask yourself why a large international cooperation would set a collaboration with such a small business. And the response is that size does not matter; interests do. The small company was able to solve some risk for the bank. In return, the bank was happy to provide them with better loans and an endless stream of clients. If you identify that you can fulfill an interest of a large organization, they would be more than happy to collaborate with you. Thus, opposed to what we described at the beginning, large businesses would demand that you do contracts properly; the collaboration is not intended for you to sell the other side a service, or that you partner toward establishing a third business together. The intention is still that you set a fruitful collaboration, fulfilling each other's interests.

Do not bother yourself with excuses; just make the right preparations and make the approach. Organizations have their own agenda and goals. They also have more tasks at hand than money, no matter how big they are. The management of such a company is well aware that not all their interests are attended to. Therefore, if you come with the right solution at the right time, they would be happy to provide you with exposure, for example. Be bold, as most of your competitors are not.

As a final note, though we now see the great benefits and probabilities deriving from setting the right collaboration, that does not mean that your negotiation partner sees it the same way. They might not be ready for such an idea. They might be overwhelmed by their tedious daily tasks, and it's impossible for them to hear new ideas right now. It may just be the wrong timing for them.

Chapter 4

Communication Tools for Success

"To effectively communicate, we must realize that we are all different in the way we perceive the world, and use this understanding as a guide to our communication with others."
– Tony Robbins

Introduction – Set the Board Game

Congratulations; you have completed the preparation stages, and you have set a meeting with that person whom you wish to collaborate with. You know your set goals, you are focused on your mission and you believe such a collaboration would get you closer to your goals.

However, it takes two to tango. If your partner has read this book, your life might be easier; but if he did not, then it's your task to set the board game. As we aim to maximize our success rate in anything we do, we have an interest that our partner in this negotiation would be as excited about the potential as we are. While we are aware that he did not invest the same amount of time preparing for this meeting as we did, we need to get him up to speed as fast and effectively as possible.

In the coming chapters, we will walk stage by stage through the WIN/WIN negotiations technique, also called interest-based negotiating, with the relevant adaptations to our goal. **Our goal is to allow small business owners and sales teams to set a fruitful collaboration with another business; a collaboration that would lead to higher sales rates and direct access to the ideal clients, while investing lower efforts and resources.**

Let's dig-in. We are now meeting for the first time with our counter partner. He is aware that we want to achieve something. We have had some earlier short conversations while setting the meeting, but he does not have the clear picture yet. We need to be aware of his position and not bombard him with our ideas yet.

We start with setting the board game, by verbalizing our guidelines. We start by sharing with him that our way of doing business is the WIN/WIN way. We continue: The WIN/WIN way does not mean that both of us get some small win, and it does not mean that both of us need to make some compromise. This is something that we have been taught, which is wrong.

The WIN/WIN strategy starts with the mutual belief that the other side is a professional. They also know the facts and what the true value is of the product or service we are discussing. We need to say out loud that we are not looking to use a sting operation on anyone, and not looking to make fast money at someone else's expense. Last but not least, I would state that I believe both of us have done our homework, and we are both aware of the market. I believe we both know what alternatives are on offer, and how these are valued.

We continue by stating that it is our intention to achieve such a result that each of us will emerge with a good feeling that he has achieved a good and honest deal. And most important, a deal that satisfies each party's business interests.

This direct statement has two roles for our future negotiation stages. First, it is relaxing our partner by saying explicitly that we have good intentions. Second, it sets the ground that we appreciate his professional know-how; and by that, it implicates that you expect him to provide you with a similar courtesy.

Learn About Your Partner

After making your little introduction speech, you need to get your partner involved. This starts with a list of small questions aimed at revealing your partner's real interests. Remember that he is not familiar with your approach so the first response you receive will probably be, "I want to make a high profit." This is not interesting; it is not an interest that will get your conversation going.

In order to assist in our progress, let us use a simple, real-life negotiation example. I am aware that this example may sound a little strange at some stages of our discussion. However, I have chosen it because it is a familiar negotiation situation for most people on the planet.

Our negotiation training example would be the sale of a second-hand car, a simple event in which I assume you possess some firsthand experience.

We just met a few minutes ago; we are both here for a simple car sale transaction. And I have already given my above WIN/WIN negotiation strategy opening. The next step is to learn about your partner's interests. In our example, we may believe he has one interest, and that is to get as high a price as possible for his car. Though that may be true, he has further interests too, and you need to discover them as soon and as clearly as possible. So I would start with general questions, such as why he is selling the car, or why this is his business. What are his business goals? What is his business path, and what is the next mission that he plans to tackle?

Be interested and listen carefully, as this is where the gold is. This is where the keys to your success lie. There are no secrets to discover here; your negotiation partner would be glad to share his goals with you, and all you need to do is listen carefully and identify which of their goals are important to them and why. Your partner has many other needs and is coping with many other difficulties, so if you wish to set a fruitful collaboration, you must be able to provide some solution to part of their needs.

Per our car sale example, I may hear that he has to offer his beloved car for sale as he needs the money to cover some loan that he took. Or maybe his daughter is about to be married, or he may need the money for some medical procedure.

Understanding his real motivation is key; if we just talk about money, all we can do is push and pull the numbers, and maybe just meet in the middle, with bad feelings on both sides.

The interests that we are looking for are called the hidden interests. For example, if he is offering his car for sale because he needs the money to finance his daughter's wedding in two weeks' time, we understand that time is of the essence. He may later be willing to drop the price a little so as to proceed with the wedding preparations. We can assess that his main interest here is to finish that transaction as soon as possible. That does not mean we will get the car for free, but it means time is of the essence.

A purchasing manager may reveal that his interest is to receive his quarterly bonus. He will disclose that he must conclude the quarter at some expansive level. That information is important for you, as you now understand that when he asks for a discount, it does not come from his wish to push you down. It actually comes from his direct interest to conclude the deal with you, and the discount you grant him will later entitle him to his bonus.

So now I know my negotiation partner is having issues with maintaining client relationship, or may wish to develop new products, or maybe he has some non-profit higher cause that he wishes to support.

What you are looking to identify are some interests that resonate with you, some interests that you feel are within your ability to offer a solution, or that you are able to assist with achieving some progress toward achieving them. Once you are able to offer progress toward achieving the other person's goals, money stops being the main issue.

Talk About Your Interests

Now that you are better friends, the other person has shared their interests and goals with you. They may even share some personal information and hidden goals, like why they need to offer their car for sale. Now it is your turn to reciprocate.

Go back to your goals and mission statement. Share why you are active in that field of business, why you have opened your business in the first place, where your business is now and what your main interests are for the near future.

Remember your preparations. You already have an idea why you are currently meeting with that person, so you do not need to overwhelm them with irrelevant information. They are not interested in your complete life story. All they want to hear is the reason why you are meeting with them, and why you believe a collaboration with you will assist them. Therefore, your information sharing has to resonate with that.

Thus, this is not a black and white scenario. People like helping other people, so sharing your interests may spark something with the other person. Maybe your goals are also important to them, or to someone very close to them. Just hearing that these are your interests and missions may cause them to want to help.

Furthermore, note that it was probable that you had not heard of all their hidden interests earlier. So now, as you reveal your interests, they may respond and say something like, "Now that you are saying …, that is also an interest of mine."

In sharing your interests, you are looking to provide stories that will resonate with the other person's interests. You are looking to excite them with the potential that someone like you will collaborate with them. Businesses usually prefer to collaborate and be associated with successful people, rather than feel they are doing you a favor. Business people would rather freely choose their donations and charities, so you do not wish to be counted as such. Your mission must excite the other person in order for them to continue setting a collaboration with you.

A further element that leads people to offer their assistance is learning that you have some big goal; that you wish to change the world, and that you take part in helping the poor or helping the planet. They may get the feeling that by collaborating with you, they are actually contributing to your cause of helping the poor. Though this is not their business goal, it is a goal they are happy to support; thus, setting the collaboration between the two businesses just became more appealing.

Assess Your Success Probability

Now that both of your interests are visible, you can assess your success probability. A negative result here will lead you to disengage, and save you a lot of time and future resources.

The object of your assessment is the collaboration. Your aim is to assess the prospect for a fruitful collaboration, a collaboration that would get you closer to your goals. You are not looking just for a nice personal relationship with the other person. You need the business collaboration to live up to your expectations.

Here are some elements you need to evaluate at this stage.

Starting with the business goals, do your business goals collide? Do you hold contrary objectives? If that is true, then this is a good time to depart. However, that is not usually the case. Your goals do not have to be similar and, in fact, it is probable that they are not. The current task is to set your inner thoughts, and construct some frame for this collaboration.

Foremost importance should be geared to your excitement. Are you feeling the excitement of collaborating with that business? Your inner intuition will automatically take into account most of the variations, so listening to your intuition is important.

However, this is your business, and though your intuition is key to your success, you need to reach a logical conclusion. The friendly person you meet may not be able to get you closer to accomplishing your goals.

Note whether their business is able to dedicate the relevant resources that will fuel your collaboration. In one instance, one of my mentees approached a collaboration with a much greater business. Our initial approach was that this company has the interest and the resources to fulfill their part in our idea for a collaboration. During the initial conversation, we discovered that all daily activities were controlled by the owner. There was very limited delegation of managerial power to other people. It was apparent that this person was so overwhelmed by the daily tasks, that there was no chance he would be able to dedicate any attention to fulfill his role in our idea for collaboration, even though the result was supposed to be very beneficial to him.

Note whether their business possesses the relevant technological tools or systems that are a key element in providing the collaboration with the elements required. In one case, I explored a collaboration with a community manager. The preliminary idea was that such a business would possess the ability to communicate with their audience through different media channels (e.g., social media, e-mails, SMS, WhatsApp groups and so on). The interest was to utilize their exposure in return for fulfilling some other interest they have revealed. However, during the initial discussion, it was revealed that they do not use any CRM technology, and all their communication was in one direction, from them to the audience via social media. As our need was for a higher level of exposure, it was apparent at an early stage that this could not be fulfilled.

Assess their business financial state. Is it able to make the investments needed? Is he looking to set a collaboration out of stress? Keep in mind that financial stress is not an automatic red indicator, even though most businesses are stressed to their limit. But this is still an important factor to consider. A person under great financial burden may not be able to dedicate any attention to your new collaboration. On the other hand, another person under the same financial burden may be highly motivated to get your collaboration going as it will assist them in solving their difficulties along the way. There is no definite response here; however, you may not neglect considering the potential effect of the other business's financial state, on their ability to take further tasks onboard.

Note the business life cycle position. A business's life cycle is an important criteria. All businesses start as a one-person idea. They later grow while making product adaptations according to market shifts. Then, after some years, they see a downfall. Revealing their current position along the timeline would reveal vital information. At one event, one of my mentees was interested in collaborating with a specific service provider. That service provider came with warm recommendations and a good reputation in his niche. Their good personal relations have led to the appearance of a nice collaboration. However, a few months into the project, when no results were registered, we set out to explore what went wrong. We noted that the other professional's business was in a very early stage. We discovered that although the guy was working as a self-employed business owner for some years. his annual income was indeed very low. He did not pass the minimum tax requirements. Per the collaboration, it became obvious that a business that has been stuck in first gear for a few years, will not be able to provide its part toward our joint project. On the other hand, discovering that the business you are approaching is pivoting to revive itself, provides great opportunities to join the ride.

Success Mindset

When embarking on a unique path to success, part of the process is to realize that your chosen path is not an obvious one. The aim of this book is to provide your business with a leading tool for success. The aim is to enable your business to benefit from a set of activities not practiced by others. The aim is to differentiate your business from the crowd of competitors. As such, it also implies that you need to change your state of mind and believe that positive possibilities are achievable.

That does not mean that you need to become a dreamer, or imagine that by tomorrow you can set a collaboration with a Hollywood film studio or with Apple Inc. It does, however, imply that you can see collaboration ideas in places other people do not. Like a muscle, we can practice and use our mind to evolve in a desired direction. Just like you cannot wake up one morning and run a marathon, you cannot expect to develop a new business mindset at one go.

Achieving a success-oriented mindset is a process for most people. It may be mastered after following set practice routines with a specific focus. Successfully accomplishing a marathon run entails an extensive period of preparation and daily routines. The same applies for evolving our mindset. We have started our journey together by setting our great unachievable goals. Then, after planning our three to five-year business path, we would detail the milestones we would need to concur. We reach a point where the earlier, unachievable goal seems achievable and even exciting.

A fixed mindset would lead you to believe that sticking to what everyone else is doing is the right thing to do; for example, investing substantial amounts into PPC (pay per click) marketing campaigns. An evolved success-oriented mind would push you to try new things, believing that failure is an opportunity to grow. The success-oriented mindset would push you to live your life believing you can become better and improve with time and practice.

Embracing a success mindset would allow you to identify new opportunities wherever you look. Each business you approach, and each person you talk to, would immediately light the collaboration opportunity bulb over your head.

A small word of caution: Your potential collaboration partner may not possess the same capability. In that case, you would need to attend to their suspicions as to the potential of them receiving that high value out of your suggested collaboration.

So, as an entrepreneur that has embarked on their unique path for success, the most important thing you can do is develop a success mindset. That is the mindset that will allow you to dream big, concur your higher goals and pull other businesses toward joining your road to success.

Set the Ground for Success

*"People should pursue what they're passionate about.
That will make them happier than pretty much anything else."*
– Elon Musk, the wealthiest person on the planet as of 2021

We are now at the stage where both you and your discussion partner have become more personally acquainted; you have set the foundations, and that is the time to add the concrete and stabilize these foundations. Earlier, we set our mindset for success; now we need to set our joined collaborative success position.

Stick to your strengths – Passion is not enough. You need to make sure that the element of your business that you intend to bring into this collaboration is one of your key strengths. The same applies to your counterparty. You need to ask the right questions to have a good understanding that the elements and tasks you plan to ask your collaboration partner to bring into the collaboration, are within the scope of their strengths. The fact that they are in a business that you think would benefit your collaboration, does not mean that they are good at it. Your mutual success depends on both of you being able to perform the relevant tasks with ease and with high proficiency.

Keep it simple – You are about to enter a potentially long-term relationship. If all goes well, both of you should be gaining from this collaboration; however, for both of you, this is not the main scope of your business. So keep it simple; do not set something that will take you too far out of your comfort zone or make things too complicated. One of the main benefits of a correct collaboration is that you gain the results with low effort and attention. That can only be achieved if the setting you made is simple enough for both of you to fulfill.

Collaborate with smarter people – In the corporate world, we identify managers that fear employing people that are smarter or more talented than them, due to their primal fear of appearing as obsolete to their peers and managers. Thus, obviously, that is a wrong corporate practice, as the higher your team's overall capabilities, the higher the levels of success that would be achieved. The same applies to your collaboration setting. Both of you have to be able to complement the deficiency of the other. This is something that you should discuss openly. No one is perfect, and neither are you. Once you share your deficiency and learn that it is exactly the strength of your collaborator, and that the same applies to them, there is a high probability that this collaboration will remain fruitful for a long period of time. Though this is not a "must" condition, and in many cases it would be hard to establish, if it does relate to you and your collaborator, it is good news for both of you.

Always add value – Never come asking for assistance. Instead, always approach with "How can I help?" It is true that your starting point is fulfilling your business needs, and that should be your internal focus. However, your collaboration partner is also focused on their business needs. For both of you to remain motivated to proceed, and for the relationship to become fruitful, they would have to see that your activity is benefiting their business. Therefore, your starting point should always be, "How can I help you?" Note that this is not only the starting point. That mutual contribution must continue throughout the life of this collaboration. Once one of the businesses feels that they are not being contributed to by the other, the collaboration will find its ending.

Chapter 5

Agreement on Facts

"Get your facts first, then you can distort them as you please." –
Mark Twain

Facts and Opinions

Are you familiar with the Manheim Used Vehicle Value Index? This index provides a value measurement scale for resold vehicles. It takes into account the brand, the age of the car and all other value relevant factors, and provides the dollar value for that specific car. I can assume a similar service exists in your country of residence.

Now let us return to our negotiation training example of the second-hand car sale. Joe is offering his family car for sale. It's a nice, three-year-old, 2.0 liter Ford Crossover, with just over 40,000 miles on its record. Its index value is just over $15,000.

David is looking for that exact same vehicle, and they meet. Joe describes his nice vehicle as a really good deal. It has no visible issues and has been taken care of with real attention, and therefore he is asking for a price that is higher than the index—he is asking for $18,000. But how does David see it? He sees it differently. David thinks, "The seller is in love with himself and the car. These days no one gets the index price, and obviously not over it. I believe that any used car has suffered some hardships; and in any case, I am limited by my actual resources. Therefore, I will not pay over $11,000; but for starters, I will offer $9,500 and see what will happen."

Sound familiar? I am sure it does.

By now, you know there is a different way that David (the buyer) can utilize for their mutual benefit. In Chapter 4, we learned that he needs to start with a small speech, setting the board game:

"I believe in the WIN/WIN way of doing business, and that means that I believe both of us have done our homework; both of us know the index value of this model, we both have no intention of making an extra-good deal by harming the other side, and we are both aware of the market. I believe we both know what alternatives are on offer, and how these are valued. Therefore, it is our intention to achieve such a result that each of us will emerge with a good feeling that he has achieved a good and honest deal."

At this stage, we pause and do not talk about money, whether we are buying or selling the product. The key for mutual success is to talk about the facts and refrain from our opinions. It does not matter how much Joe is in love with his car, and there is no importance to David's belief that any used car must have suffered some hardship. It does not matter how much you love the service you provide. All these are under our "opinion" category. We will take these into consideration later. But at this stage, we need to focus the discussion only on the facts.

A fact is something that exists in reality, which can be measured and proven. In our negotiation training example, the facts will include the vehicle model, age, physical condition, mileage and so on.

When setting a collaboration, the WIN/WIN or the interest-based negotiating methodology does not change. We need to set the facts clearly, if you wish to set a collaboration for marketing purposes and to rely on the other party to extend your brand exposure. The facts may include the size of their database, how involved their database members are with them, whether they have experience in promoting other businesses, and whether they have had incidents involving complaints that they are marketing other products or services too heavily. All these are facts you both have to reveal. As stated already, neither of you wish any harm to the other.

Fact Assessment

Once all facts are revealed, we have to join hands and assess their importance and relevancy to both of us. For example, the fact that the car is red may or may not be important to the buyer. Establishing that the car is red is simple. However, most of the facts in the business arena are harder to establish.

When we embark on setting a collaboration between two businesses, we have some positive pictures in mind. Now is the time to assess its match with reality. If our intention is to set a collaboration with a celebrity, where their contribution would be exposure of our brand, this is the stage we ask for their database information, how large their audience is, and through which media channels they communicate with their audience. Are they responsive to their audience, or maybe it is a one-way channel. Do they just post pictures or do they respond to audience comments too? What are their audience's characteristics—age, sex, married or single, economic status and so on—as they relate to your service or product.

The same applies to the service you wish to bring into the collaboration. The fact that they appreciate your input is important, but your partner will have to hear what your input is and agree to its relevancy. Furthermore, giving your input at this stage will contribute to the overall atmosphere of participating in a good business collaboration.

My earlier homework revealed that this TikTok celebrity had suffered some loss following an accident. They are now involved in some charity work, assisting in bringing attention to safety. Since my service is focused on accident rehabilitation, the facts may be that the treatment methods I practice have been proven to assist in rehabilitation, or that the product I wish to promote reduces the accident risk, or the accident impact. The facts will also include the size of my organization, the geographical availability of my service and so on.

I would detail any facts that may be relevant to my collaboration partner. Because I have some predetermined idea in mind, I would lay down all the facts that would establish the relevance of my contribution to the other person's interest if I am planning to offer some donation out of any deal that may result due to that celebrity's publication. By that, I mean expanding her contribution to that charity. I would present my plan as offering that by collaborating with me, the charity she supports would not only gain her publicity exposure but also get direct donations from my business. Therefore, relevant facts would be how much money could be donated due to the growth of my business, my business's good reputation, reports of client satisfaction rates and so on.

Following the discovery of our mutual information, we would together have to present our opinion as per the other party's fact. Each side may state that some facts are not relevant for him. As you are leading the process, you may have to educate your discussion partner that some statements made are their opinions rather than measurable facts.

At this stage, all that has to occur is that we have to assess the relevancy of the facts to our negotiation. Remember that my liking of the car being red is not relevant right now, only that it is red.

Set Fact Hierarchy

By now, the mutual presentations have been revealed. Each party has detailed a lot of information. As the information accumulates, we need to prioritize what is most important and influential for the transaction value, and what is mere information that does not influence the transaction.

Note that the issue at hand is only setting the factual hierarchy. Only at a later stage would we explore what interests are important to each party.

Returning to our used car negotiation, the discussion will now focus on setting an agreement relating to what facts are important and which are negligible (i.e. obviously, at the top, we would set the vehicle's model and production year). But what about the vehicle's color? For some people, that is the most negligible fact; for others, this is a very important issue. All other facts must also be placed on the gauge we are building. Note that we are not negotiating what the value reduction is for that scratch on the door. All we need to accomplish is an agreement on what elements are more important and which are less important. So, the fact that the car is three years old is an important fact. After a short discussion, you may agree that the fact that the car is white is of no real importance to either of you. In the same way, you need to set the hierarchy for the remaining facts. The importance of the external physical condition may be higher in relation to the importance of the interior condition. The engine condition will receive a higher level of importance, and so on.

This is an important exercise for several reasons. It will assist in reducing the influence of psychological duress over the negotiations. As we set the facts in order, we are pushed to give less attention to our feelings. That is true for both persons, so the fact that the seller loves his car and thinks it's the best becomes less influential. It will take its effect via the facts, so if he loves his car, and therefore the car was treated well and is in great condition, we would account for that as a fact.

If our collaborator has a large client list, but they never communicate with their database, we would have to agree about the level of importance of that database. Therefore, we may state that their popularity on social media is an important fact, while the fact that their store client database was never approached takes this database down the hierarchy.

As the purpose of this book is to walk you through the collaboration path to success, as per this stage of the discussion, it means to focus on the facts that are relevant for the collaboration. There is no intension for either of the collaborating parties to invest in the other. Therefore, there is no need to embark on a full due-diligence process. Concentrate only on the facts that are relevant toward the success of the collaboration.

There is a saying, "There is no bad publicity," and it implies that any media exposure is good for business. However, maybe the other party's bad publicity will rub off on your brand once you collaborate, so you may wish to grant it higher importance than they do. Now is the time to agree how influential it is for your transaction or collaboration.

Assess Facts – Interest Correlation

The business goals should always be visible at any stage. That implies that the main purpose of setting this transaction or setting that collaboration is to fulfill a pre-determined business objective.

Any fact that would get us closer to our goals is an important one. Therefore, we need to correlate the above facts with our business interests. As per our used car example, if David (the buyer) had detailed that his interest was to buy a second family car, intended for short in-town errands, that may imply that the high mileage registered with the seller's car is of less importance to him. The same interest would also correlate with the car's interior condition, as the buyer's interest is that the kids would be comfortable at the back.

Some facts may not correlate with any of your interests; thus, unless you give them some general positive score, they would become irrelevant, while you may discover new facts that suddenly greatly influence your interests.

If a political party wishes to collaborate with some employee organization, their general interest is clear: They wish to increase their support group. The employee organization interest may be to get greater government support in the future, or it could be to get closer to job opportunities, etc. However, during discussions, they reveal that one of the key persons at that employee organization has some skeletons in their closet. He has a bad reputation.

The new information is not an opinion; it is a fact. As such, they would need to assess its impact on their interests. Earlier, they did not look to increase the political party's good reputation via this collaboration. However, now they would need to enter into their considerations another interest that they hold. Like all political players, they obviously have an interest in good reputation. Now they will have to assess if that new fact may harm their good-reputation interest. Later, in Chapter 6, we will pause on the importance of listening to the other person. For now, we need to note that new information that we did not consider may become very important.

Agree on the Facts

The last task in our fact finding mission is to reach an agreement on the facts. That may sound obvious, but it is not. The agreement on the fact takes place before we even talk about money or the product's value. Now that we have examined the product and listened to its description, we need to make sure we are both looking the same way at the same product.

As per our vehicle example, we need to both agree that we consider the tire condition in the same way, refraining from a situation whereby one looks at the tires and sees tires that are in good condition and will hold for the coming few years, while the other looks at the same tires and thinks they need to be replaced immediately as currently they should be considered a risk.

Agreement on Facts

The agreement on the facts is a vital element in the WIN/WIN negotiation technique. By now, you should already notice the future impact the facts have on reducing the attention that both sides give to their opinions. However, that would become a negotiation tool only after you reach an agreement on the facts. If the car buyer sees the tire condition as requiring immediate replacement, then he would wish to take that fact into consideration when setting the car's value; while if the seller does not consider that investment necessary, he would be reluctant to lower his asking value.

Alternatively, if they reach an agreement on facts, and if they both agree that the tire condition is relatively fine, then later on, they would refrain from the value argument, at least per that agreed issue.

It is worth your while to invest as much time as seems necessary to resolve any issue relating to the fact, and have an understanding of both sides. Achieving an equal understanding of the simple facts resolves future negotiations and misunderstandings even before they occur.

If necessary, you may agree that you would need some external expert to assess some facts. In that case, your task at this stage is to reach an agreement relating to the identity of that person, and that any decision that person makes is accepted by both of you upfront. For example, David, our vehicle buyer, would like to know what the engine condition is. Once both agree that this is a relevant fact to the transaction, they would be wise to agree to have the car examined, while agreeing upfront to accept the examiner's comments relating to the engine as an agreed fact.

Earlier, we noted the Manheim Used Vehicle Value Index. The same index idea exists in many business fields. The index is also a tool that could be used in reaching agreements relating to facts. In many cases, just agreeing on the facts becomes a great challenge, as it is clear to both parties that any fact description will later have some value impact. It may cause the seller not to agree that the tires are old, and the buyer would try to refrain from agreeing that the vehicle is in mint condition. However, our task is to walk both parties down the WIN/WIN path for a successful deal closure. That implies that they be honest and appreciate the effort the other side is making to be just as honest. For that, using an agreeable index may assist both to set an agreeable value for the facts at hand. If the vehicle index does not rate the color as an element that is value relevant, than both should agree that the red car is just a red car. If the buyer does not like the color, he does not have to proceed with the deal, but if he does proceed with the negotiations, then the color is not an interest that could be addressed as a value factor. The opinion he has against that color does not make any difference any longer.

When approaching our collaboration partner, we need to forgo the exact same negotiation path. In that case, the facts may be more elusive than identifying the tire condition or the car color. However, revealing them is important just the same. When

Agreement on Facts

approaching a public relations company, I would look to their past clientele list and explore the correlation between their past experience and the role I would like them to take in our collaboration. The description that says they have great experience in helping entrepreneurs raise investments, may be registered as per our collaboration-building discussion, as a fact relating to their ability to get media exposure. At the same time, the same description may lead to a different fact: that they have no experience in talking to small businesses—same activity description, two different facts. If my collaboration mission is to increase the exposure of my services toward my target market of small businesses, then we both will have to agree if I value their ability to get media exposure as important, or if our collaboration would require approaching the small business communities; and in that case, the fact is that they have no experience.

The requirement for mutual agreement here relates to the wish we both have to make that collaboration a mutually beneficial one. Therefore, there is no benefit in convincing that some ability exists when it does not, as it will backfire later, and both parties will lose time and money.

Chapter 6

Communicating Toward Agreement

"Unless both sides win, no agreement can be permanent."
– President Jimmy Carter

Reaffirm the WIN/WIN Method

By now, you are very close to finalizing the collaboration. By now, you should have a clear picture in your mind whether this person is the right collaborator partner for your business.

At this stage, I would like to pause for a short break, and we will proceed toward closing the collaboration in the next chapter. Right now, I would like us to pause and elaborate a little on the importance of using the right communication patterns. That pause is crucial for the setting of a fruitful collaboration, as the whole idea is to lead both persons into a long relationship. The distinction between the collaboration situation and the setting of a legal partnership between two companies is essentially that the partnership agreement would usually involve mutual investments, and the process itself will involve a greater number of people. The implication is that the partnership is not a one-on-one relationship;

thus, the lawyers will make sure that the agreements are protecting your interests, the sales people or the engineers are doing their part and so on. However, the collaboration between two small businesses is 100% dependant on the relationship developed by the two collaborating persons.

As such, any hours invested in reaffirming the intentions and the capabilities, at early stages, will save great amounts of money and efforts at later stages.

The basis of a long-lasting collaboration remains as discussed earlier: a successful result of a WIN/WIN negotiation done right. Until now, we have set the ground by uniting two negotiation approaches. At first, we clearly identified that this potential collaboration would get us closer toward our goals by fulfilling one of our upcoming missions. This was an internal stage toward our success. Second, we made sure both parties were on the same page, both agreeing as to the reality of their starting point. Both reached a similar understanding of the baseline and have agreed on the facts. By now, the risk of surprises is very low. The next stage would be to explicitly detail the way you see the collaboration materializing.

Many times, the personal communication will deteriorate, especially during the discussions relating to fact presentation and examination. Specifically, when one person has the expectation that some fact would strengthen his pricing position, discussion over that element may become very emotional. Therefore, my approach is to conclude the fact finding dissection with a little break, making sure both of us reaffirm that we come with best intentions and wish to conclude a jointly fruitful negotiation, achieving a WIN/WIN result.

Again, this has to be said verbally. It is your responsibility to make sure your negotiation partner is reminded of your initial agreement: the agreement stating you both appreciate each other as honest people, both hold the belief that the other person has done his homework, and that both have no intention of leading the other toward something that will harm them.

Like before, this pause and verbal communication of the WIN/WIN negotiation technique holds the power to relax both you and the other person simultaneously. It will also provide an opportunity for the other person to raise any issue that although discussed earlier, he may still be unhappy with in regard to the way it was concluded. Allowing such issues to be resolved before you start negotiating the deal itself, increases the success chances of your negotiations.

Merge Interests with the Facts

Maslow's hierarchy of needs is a well-known examination tool for identifying the attention a client would give to a product or a service. The higher the need you are solving, the greater the attention your service or product will attract. Attending to the physiological needs is the basis for anything (food, sleep, clothing), while the top of Maslow's hierarchy of needs includes the need for self-actualization (i.e. the desire to become the best you can be).

During the WIN/WIN negotiation technique, our goal is to attend to both persons' interests as best we can. There must not be winners and losers, just the vision of fulfilling the maximum interests of both persons. Thus, we should be aware that fulfilling all interests is an unachievable target. Therefore, there is a need to prioritize the interest. Some facts are not open for interpretation;

thus, we should just examine if we are okay with them or not. For example, a red car is a red car; there is no room for opinions here. However, the physical condition of the rear seat is open for interpretation. If the buyer is a young person, say a twenty-year-old student, he may not consider some interior issues of the rear seat. For him, the exterior of the car is more important. However, if the buyers are a young couple, raising two very young kids, the condition of the rear seat is rated as a higher interest for them, while the exterior condition may be placed lower along their list of interests.

When setting a collaboration with a public relations company, my interest may be to get maximum exposure; so the fact that they have 5 years' experience may potentially fulfill my mission to increase my exposure. Thus, if my interest is for publicity toward a specific audience, the same experience may not merge with my interests, and I will need to know that during their five years of activity they have approached my targeted audience with success.

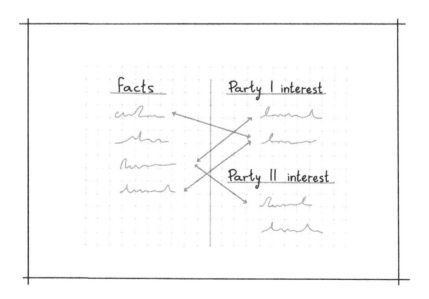

The correlation between the facts we have gathered, facts relating to both of us and our separate interests, is the reason we have started our negotiation with a fact-finding exercise. Our current goal is to make sure our interests are being addressed by the other partner's abilities while making sure they are happy to contribute these abilities toward our collaboration. As this understanding may come to you naturally as reasonable, I would like to direct you to make sure the contrary also applies, and that the abilities you are happy to bring to the collaboration, actually correspond with the other person's interests. In fact, it is more important for you to satisfy the other person's interests than it is for you to satisfy all your interests.

Note that your ability to set fruitful collaborations is a great tool that your competitors do not have. Therefore, in cases where you conclude that this specific collaboration fulfills only part of your interests but not all of them, you hold the ability to set another parallel collaboration aimed at fulfilling the remaining of your interests, while making sure that this collaboration does continue to fulfill part of your interests for as long as possible. That could only be achieved as long as your collaborator feels that his interests are well addressed by your collaboration, which means that your interest in the long survival of this collaboration becomes a key interest by itself. That interest will only be addressed by making sure that your partner in the collaboration is happy that his interests are fulfilled. Therefore, your main interest is that they are happy. If needed, you can set another parallel collaboration with some other business to fulfill any further interests you have and that are not attended by the current collaboration you are setting now.

Once the facts, as agreed, hold the potential of fulfilling even part of your interests, thus getting you closer to your goals, the collaboration setting is still moving in the right direction for you.

Assess Correlation of Interests

Earlier, we prioritized our interests; now we can correlate these with our potential partner's interests, with a clear intention of fulfilling the higher interests first. This may not always be so straightforward, and as a businessperson, you should be ready for some flexibility.

While setting our missions toward achieving our goals, we used the example of the family weekend trip to Niagara Falls. We talked about the situation, where it was discovered that some road interference would cause us a ninety-minute delay, and we were flexible enough to choose a different route. The same applies here; we may discover that some interests we have aimed for are not achievable via this collaboration. The facts just do not lead toward the ability of fulfilling all our interests.

When planning our move, we had a set plan in mind, leading us toward a happy mission fulfillment. Sometimes that is exactly the way things would turn out. However, on other occasions, we may discover that our partner's interests are either far from what we imagined, or even conflicting with our own interests.

In one instance, I worked with a business-tutoring firm. We had approached a celebrity with a plan to involve him as a guest in one of the seminars. The pre-planned idea was based on the understanding that his media activity was in some way close to that of the same targeted audience, though not exactly directly. Gathering the relevant publications, we assessed that he had an interest in expanding his visibility toward that same audience, leading us to conclude that there was some prospected opportunity for a WIN/WIN collaboration. Upon conducting our discussion, as we were presenting the mutual interests, it was revealed that he did have that interest in his list of objectives, but his other interest was conflicting with the tutoring firm.

Revealing that conflict of interest at an early stage saves you time and money associated with the preparation of an elaborated proposal.

On the other hand, it provides new opportunities. The revealing of a conflict of interest may seem to shut the door on the collaboration opportunity. However, if you discover it at this early stage, before placing your offer on the table, you may turn the conversation around. You could now utilize the good relationship that was set, to ask for the other person's thoughts on how you may collaborate. You would be surprised that their new ideas may solve your interests from a different angle. The board game was set in such a manner that both sides learn and get closer to each other simultaneously. By that, it allows you to navigate the conversation from your original plan toward asking the other person for their ideas, or maybe just for a referral to a friend of theirs, where the interests would not contradict. They would usually be happy to assist.

By now, they also are aware of your interests, and as you have already set the WIN/WIN relationship, they would not like to lose that opportunity either. Talking only about facts and interests, rather than jumping into talking about money from the start, has set the ground for joint flexibility.

The advantage and flexibility the collaboration solution provides the businesses participating, includes the non-exclusive relationship. Since we probably have a list of several interests to fulfill, we may discover that the collaboration we planned is not going toward the same conclusive direction we hoped. However, with minor adjustments, we can utilize it to fulfill other objectives.

Therefore, it is recommended to set the right adjustments, fulfill our relevant objectives and continue searching for a second collaboration, one that would satisfy the remaining interests in our original plan.

Talk-Listen Ratio

"We have two ears and one mouth so that we can listen twice as much as we speak," is a quote attributed to Epictetus, a Greek philosopher. This old and smart proverb intends to highlight the correct behavior for human interaction.

The ultimate business goal is to generate income. In fast moving economies, we have learned that the salespersons are the most important people in the company as they bring in the money. In addition, the automatic sales technique would include passing as much information toward your client so that he has no questions and places an order, just like it has been happening in street markets for millennia.

When paraphrasing that understanding into our small business, we inevitably set a nice presentation detailing all our service's or product's benefits, and why we believe it is the best.

Epictetus wishes to teach us something else. He wants us to return to the basics, to stop pushing ourselves and to start building relationships with our audience. This new idea came up a few years before social media and storytelling. Epictetus was active around the year 100 A.D.

Contrary to speaking, listening seems to be a passive activity. You are only listening. However, in many cases, the power of listening is greater than the power of speech. Human relationships are based on listening, between couples, parents and children, friends, etc. The basis for human relationships is listening. We are aware that our listeners may not agree with us, but we still ask them to listen. Not paying attention correlates with impatience and disrespect, while getting the feeling that our discussion partner is listening to us leads to the perception that they care, thus creating a positive relationship.

This is not only a perception exercise. We have dedicated a substantial part of the WIN/WIN methodology to listening to the other person's needs and interests. That does not imply that we must fulfill all their needs. However, it does set the board game for a relationship that would serve both of the collaborators toward getting closer to achieving their goals.

People would buy a product from, or collaborate with, people they like. Since people like to be heard, it satisfies their ego, and it makes the speaker feel important. Therefore, if you make me feel important, there are higher chances that I will like you; thus, the road for sales or for setting any relationship is open. It has been said that we were given two ears and one mouth because it is twice as hard to listen as it is to talk.

It is worth investing the time for stressing that there is a difference between hearing and listening. Listening means paying attention and making a conscious effort to process what you hear. Listening is a skill that should be developed. It stands contrary to our basic need to be heard, especially for entrepreneurs. The enthusiasm for the service or product drives entrepreneurs to elaborate more and more.

When listening to the other person's description of their interests, make a conscious effort to listen. Listen to how their tone changes, and identify what is more important to them. Be patient and let the other person complete their sentences; only then ask questions intended to make sure you understand the speaker. Try to understand the speaker's point of view and why they believe these interests are important to their higher goal. Try to understand the speaker's feelings.

It is worth noting that the success of the WIN/WIN negotiation process relies heavily on the ability to pay attention to the other person's needs and interests. That is why it is also called interest-based negotiating: offering a path to fulfilling their interests through collaborating with you. Note that all that occurs before you get to a product value assessment (i.e. before you start negotiating the price).

Talk About the Interests and Values

We have invested a substantial part of this book in talking about identifying your interests and values, while almost ignoring the pricing of the products or services. You may assume that this is intentional. The negotiation term for the price is "position," and while we may find common ground when exploring our mutual interests, there is a very small chance of finding common ground when each side holds their position. The position is the explicit amount demanded or offered for a product, while the interest is the verbal description of why a person is interested in that transaction.

For example, let us return to our negotiation training example of the second-hand car sale. In Chapter 5, Joe is offering his family car for sale. He is asking for $18,000, and David offers to buy it at $9,500. The chance of these two closing a deal looks very slim. Each would try holding his position longer, and the gap would eventually send them in different directions. However, talking about the interest would lead the seller to say, "I want to get as much money as I can for this car," or "I want to get the best market value I can get"; while the buyer would say, "I want to pay as little as possible, relating to the vehicle market value." That sounds totally different, correct?!

As a rule of thumb, if a specific name or number is mentioned, it is a position.

You have probably noticed that when talking about interests, we have managed to draw lists of interests of both persons. The same would apply to any negotiation. People have many interests, and there are usually several ways to satisfy each interest, and only one way to satisfy a position. The variety of alternatives is the ground floor for the interest-based negotiation, or the WIN/WIN technique. As our teaching relies on your role as the leading person, it is your role to become as innovative and creative as possible when searching for alternative solutions to satisfy both your interests and your counterparty's interests.

Note that a good WIN/WIN solution may result in you compromising your position while fulfilling your interest in some other way. In our second-hand car sale negotiation training example, your interest as a buyer included rear seats suitable for your children. Imagine the seller is the proud owner of a youth education business, which you learned while conducting the initial discussion. Therefore, you may choose to ask if he is willing to accept your son into one of his programs. This may lead you to increase your offer for the car, and you may move your position closer to his. The fact that the other person may fulfill a different interest of yours, has just increased the way you see the value of the transaction.

A WIN/WIN solution based on these interests has just closed the deal even before you negotiated the numbers. Accepting another kid into the youth programs, at minimal cost, may be an easy task for that person, while it serves his interest of "getting as high a price as possible for the car." Since your family budget has already accounted for an afternoon program for your child, the same amount could go toward the car value, as long as it was reduced from the price you would pay for the said tuition. Coming with an open mind may lead you to increase the offer you intended to state. That same principle goes in both directions; it may also get the other person closer to your position.

Make sure to keep the conversation courteous, and avoid attributing blame. Stick to the interests, and make sure everyone knows that their interests are considered. Once their interests are addressed, people are more likely to be receptive to different points of view.

People are seldom stubborn just for the sake of it, and there are almost always real and valid differences behind conflicting positions. The way that each person sees the issue may be influenced by many factors, such as their values, beliefs, status, responsibilities and cultural backgrounds.

For example, a salesperson may seem stubborn when asked for a discount, only because this deal may lead him to cross his sales targets, entitling him to a nice bonus. Understanding his interest may reveal that your interests are not conflicting. You may suggest that if the deal were dated now, he would get the bonus, and he may have the flexibility to receive the payment at a later date. While your interest is to limit your expenses during this month, you have no problem paying the difference in two months' time. The discovery of both sides' interests has solved the differences in the pricing position, while fulfilling both persons' interests.

Assess the Opportunity

Once business people set their minds that collaborations are a useful tool in assisting with their business growth, collaboration ideas and opportunities will start popping up like mushrooms after the rain. That is good news; however, no one has the time and resources to invest in exploring all opportunities. For that reason, it is vital to set a defined system and method for assessing each opportunity that may look relevant.

Opportunity assessment is the process of identifying and screening project ideas. Selected collaborations should align with and support your predefined goals and objectives.

Opportunities possess the power of drawing our resources toward a better future. As much as our entrepreneur spirit may be drawn by an opportunity, we must always keep our objectives in mind.

Implementing a structured process of examining ideas will target our limited resources to those ideas with the highest business potential.

When considering a collaboration that would take two to tango, much of the assessment would have to become a joint process before initiating the collaboration.

The collaboration opportunity assessment process is composed of three elements:

1. The collaboration idea generation
2. The collaboration structuring and agreement
3. Collaboration initiation

The idea may have generated in the privacy of your business, or may have been generated by your potential collaborator. At this stage, we are not interested in the original idea generation process; you are now facing a specific collaboration opportunity. Each person, each business and each opportunity is different. Therefore, the specific collaboration opportunity has to be assessed as per the specific facts and interests it should fulfill for both collaborators. Hence, the idea generation would be the specific collaboration as was discussed during the earlier part of the mutual business interest descriptions.

The purpose of this assessment stage is to discover and present—first to yourself and later to the other person—the understanding of the correlation between the opportunity and your business interests, while making sure that the other person's business interests are also promoted by the same collaboration opportunity.

The collaboration structuring may be promoted by one of the collaborators. However, it is a mutual process. Each potential collaborator should be able to specify what tasks and action items would come under his responsibility, while also being able to assess that the other party's responsibilities contribute to the joint progression of both collaborators. In assessing the collaboration opportunity, we do need to see that all tasks could be synchronized, keeping in mind that the mutual interests are also promoted.

If it is revealed that the task structuring is not synchronized, it is a red flag, indicating that proceeding with such a collaboration effort may just not be worth the attention. Thus, if it is revealed that both collaborators are aligned in their vision of the tasks that should be performed, and both see the results as bringing them closer to their mission fulfillments and goals, such an understanding is a great indicator that this is a great opportunity.

Following the mutual positive assessment of the collaboration opportunity, an agreement should be noted. At this stage, I am not referring to the final collaboration agreement, but rather the mutual acceptance by both parties that the opportunity is positively accepted by both.

Once you are satisfied that this collaboration opportunity holds the potential of fulfilling your business missions, the next stage would be the initiation of the project, as elaborated in Chapters 6 and 7 of this book.

Assess Your Partner

In assessing the opportunity, we have learned that it is beneficial to conduct a joint assessment, and the final assessment stage was to reach an agreement relating to the opportunity, and progress toward its initiation. However, another process has to take place, which may be conducted in parallel to earlier assessments, or you may choose to conduct it in the privacy of your home. In any case, it is an important stage that deserves your attention.

Before finalizing the collaboration, you need to assess that your collaborator is the right person and business for the task ahead. You need to make sure you believe that collaborating with that person can get you closer to your goals.

In assessing your partner, it is recommended to use a mixed method approach, which means to use a combination of quantitative (numbers, measurable data) and qualitative (brand value perception, communication quality, opinions and ideas) data. Combining these two approaches provides the "numbers" to justify the collaboration, with the deeper understanding of "why" and "how." Understanding your potential collaborator's way of business would justify the efforts and skills required to be invested by you, toward the project's success.

Focusing on evaluating the collaborator's business and personal attributes, would start by determining what evaluation questions you should ask, and deciding how and when you will collect your data.

Considering that task, you can start developing questions that will assist in the evaluation process. Qualitative or personal characteristics may include elements such as leadership, resources, characteristics of their team members, their business position elements, their market share, their defined purpose and objectives, media communication practices and even the decision-making processes.

Evaluating the quantitative aspects would include getting information such as the number of social media followers; the percentage of followers that are responsive to their communications; size of the database; the number of monthly communications they send to their database, and the interactions these receive; the number of employees; years of experience and so on.

After you have developed a list of evaluation questions, prioritize which are more important for you to respond to. Rank them based on the questions most important to you in regard to the specific objective that this collaboration should fulfill in your business path. The "must answer" questions are those that provide you with the items that would progress your business, or those that are crucial for your brand regardless of this specific collaboration, like making sure your brand is contributed to by this collaborator's reputation.

Assessing your partner also includes assessing the effort you would need to make in order to satisfy their hopes and objectives. You need to determine the feasibility of your resource investment in the collaboration. This stage includes identifying gaps in your work activity, determining what action items you will need to take, and asking yourself if you are willing to produce the results that would be required by the other person so that they fulfill their goals. To assess the political and social context in which the collaboration will operate, this stage will include the assessment of the vision, mission and core strategy for forming the collaboration.

When more than two businesses take part in the same collaboration, all the above assessments have to be conducted, both separately and in relation to each business, and for the overall collaboration, including all participants.

In many cases, a fruitful collaboration would include a triangle of interest fulfilling. For example, when "A" and "B" are engaged in one relationship, and the result actually supports the interest of "C," who in turn helps "A" in fulfilling his goals. Such an example would be discussed in Chapter 7. At this stage, it suffices to say that usually this would make the collaboration even stronger, though it may take longer to establish.

Chapter 7

Suggest the Collaboration

"Collaboration is the best way to work. It's the only way to work, really. Everyone's there because they have a set of skills to offer across the board."
— Antony Starr

Starting with the Big Mission

All is ready for your collaboration. You have that gut feeling that this should work just fine, and you are already feeling the good vibes of mission accomplishment. That will follow the success of this new collaboration. Before reaching the deal closure stage, there is a last need to verify that the collaboration will fulfill its role in your business path.

Whenever introducing new people to the business, there is a need to brand yourself in the best way possible so that the relationship would be set from the start in the right frame, and this collaboration is no exception. The person introduced to a business is actually also asking himself why you are doing what you are doing, and why you have taken it upon yourself to open this business or to offer that service.

Showing that you are aware of what is happening inside their head, is also serving your mission of strengthening the new relationship. The branding of your business is also the face you would like this collaborator to see. You have probably invested in sharpening your brand appearance and messages, so now is the time to show your brand with glory.

Any relationship starts slowly, step-by-step. You first took your spouse out for coffee, and then to a movie or a show, and slowly the relationship was built. The same would also apply to this collaboration. The person that seems to be happy to set this collaboration with your business, has his or her own hidden doubts and worries. That is understandable and positive, as you would expect a good businessperson to be careful with their reputation and business name; thus, their worrying mean that you are dealing with a good businessperson. However, as we are aware of their thoughts, we had better respond and provide them with the best answer to soothe their worries.

The best soothing response you have is your branding material and story, which is your big mission. Your big mission is why you have started with your activity. I believe the answer is not just to make big money, but rather something that indicates a higher cause. For example, Satya Nadella, Microsoft's CEO, declares that Microsoft's goal is to empower every person and organization in the world with technology. Yes, as you know, they are making nice money too. But if you consider collaborating with a person, would you not rather hear that they are on a mission to empower people? Nadella also makes sure that when they embark on developing new technologies, they have another objective in mind. For him, empathy is a guideline. He says, "The source of innovation comes from having a deep sense of empathy."

Now, if a giant like Microsoft introduces themselves as being driven by empathy to empower people, then what about you? Should you be hesitant in declaring that you have started your business with a higher mission?

What was Ford's mission? To sell many cars and make a lot of money? No. Ford's mission was, "Opening the highways to all mankind." When this is your goal, then you can make people join your quest for bettering the world.

We are referring to our first chapter. Your larger goal possesses the power to assist in this collaboration, getting it started with the right foot forward.

Earlier, you and your potential collaborator revealed your interests, leading you to the understanding that collaborating with that person holds the power to assist you in fulfilling your missions. Now, as you step toward finalizing the deal toward setting the collaboration, it is the right time to tighten the knot. It is the right time to make sure the momentum is strong. That can be achieved by highlighting your greater goal and making sure your collaborator is also passionate about your business goal, or at least is happy to take part in getting you closer to that goal. A relationship based on a big mission will develop faster and produce better results.

Set Mutual Trust

A few years back, a client of mine, operating in the food industry, received a call from a foreign food distribution company. He was happy to learn that they had identified his products as being interesting for their market. He examined their minimal website, and after a short period of time, he was notified that the company's owner would like to be invited to visit their production facility. Obviously, motivation and hopes were high. Contracting with a foreign distributor, and being able to present their products in foreign food chains, would be a great opportunity. The distributor came for a visit; they had a few meetings, toured the facility and an agreement was signed. Unfortunately, once the visit had ended, the person disappeared.

For our purposes, we may guess that there were some undisclosed interests for that visit. That did not include the fulfillment of that agreement. But we can also learn another lesson from this event: Even though they were both nice people, trust was not achieved.

One of the greatest barriers in establishing a "fruitful collaboration" is setting mutual trust. Trust is a fundamental component for a collaboration's success, but it is hard to attain. This is because the collaboration is set in a space where the hierarchy is undefined, and not all is under your control. Further-more, the collaboration demands personal investment, while the reward is sometimes unclear.

Our first inclination is to doubt any message we hear. In today's digital world, setting up a nice website and producing a high-level digital appearance is much easier than it was in the past. That holds two implications for small businesses. First, branding a small business just became much easier and requires lower investment. But the second implication is that people are reluctant in offering their trust. It is much harder today to gain trust; however, it is as important as it ever was.

Thus, with the right glasses, this obstacle is also a great opportunity. If trust has become such a rare commodity, then once you gain a person's trust, be it a client or a business collaborator, that person is yours for life. Meaning, if trusting a business is such a bother, then people would rather avoid the hassle. In today's world, once a person trusts a business, they are reluctant to search and explore the competitors, and are happy with their choice of trust. That is both a marketing opportunity and a tool to increase the productivity of the new collaboration.

Trust is not a marketing trick. It is a key for building lasting relationships. Building trust is like building a friendship. Start with your commonalities and your joint interests; show empathy to your collaborator's interests, and develop from there.

Showing that you do not take their trust for granted goes a long way in gaining a person's trust. Building trust with a potential collaborator is very similar to trust building as required toward clients. Clients' or business partners' video testimonials are an important tool. The collaborator would examine your business just as if he were a client, even though he has no intention to buy your service. A video testimonial stating that you or your product are good at what you are offering, and testifying that dealing with you was a pleasant experience, would go a long way.

A written review from other clients, which can be presented in proximity to a video testimonial, will help strengthen the video effect. This written evidence should also be presented on open platforms like social media, so as to reduce the skepticism of the new listener.

A further trust-building tool is your brand appearance. Earlier, we noted that people are now skeptical of online presentations; nevertheless, people would rather collaborate with a high-quality-appearing brand. A professional website design that is simple to navigate, is optimized for mobile devices and has clear texts and relevant graphics, are all trust-building tools.

Like any issue discussed in this book, this is a double-edged sword. In the same way it is important for you to gain your discussion partner's trust, it is also important that you examine and consider whether you are happy to grant your trust, and to make sure this is a good person with whom to join for the long run.

Detail Your Contribution

It is obvious that you enter the collaboration setting due to your goals and objectives, while the other side of the same coin is that your potential collaborator will have their own reasons for exploring this collaboration. Their decision will come only when they are happy that this joint project will benefit them in some influential manner. Hence, they must achieve a clear conviction that you are able and willing to assist them in progressing their interests.

The best way to embark on that task is to conduct your research before even making the initial approach. Once you have identified some higher goal that this person is aiming for, it is your role to decide if and how you would like—or whether you are able—to contribute to their agenda.

A well-designed collaboration will be based on symmetry; each must feel that he has contributed to the same extent as the other, taking into account the different market share each holds.

The response to acknowledging your collaborator's standing, is the detailing of your contribution to them; not your contribution to the collaboration, as the collaboration does not have a life of its own. They are interested to hear how your actions would contribute to their business, thus making this part of your presentation a crucial element for your success.

Suggest the Collaboration

Start with your assumption of their relevant goals as you understand them, and wait for a confirmation. Once you are clear that you got it right, start with elaborating why you believe this collaboration will strengthen their market positioning or their personal and business interests. As you draw the new picture for them, and you listen to clarify, you are on the right path. Now comes the time to hammer the final nail. Elaborate as much as possible why your actions would progress their interests, while providing good reasoning why this is also important for you. As your discussion partner would have his internal reservations, as we all do, they are looking to hear that you have your own reason why you would like to invest resources in helping them with their goals. This is understandable and expected; therefore, resonating with their thoughts is important for your success.

While detailing your contribution to their goals, it is important to obtain symmetry of effort. At this stage, you may be eager to get this collaboration running, as you have your own goals in mind. However, the collaboration success is measured by the duration of its existence. Hence, it is important to set some correlation between your effort investment and theirs. The symmetry of invested contribution is the key for the longevity of this collaboration. For businesspersons, that understanding comes natural with experience. Your partner is looking to hear your enthusiasm toward helping them reach their goals; however, they are also looking to hear that your efforts have some correlation to their contribution toward your interests. The symmetry of the relationship will increase the chances for success.

Make sure your offered actions and contribution toward their interests are doable for you, are reasonably achievable and would resonate with setting a symmetry that would communicate what you are hoping they will do for you.

Detail Your Needs

The second side of the same discussion is making sure your collaborator understands your needs. Business activity is derived by the wish to generate wealth, and you may assume your partner understands that. The final activity in a business is the sales of products and services, thus creating the aimed wealth. However, as was elaborated earlier, the business path progresses via a list of objectives, missions and tasks. While it is reasonable to assess that the potential collaborator understands that your business is looking to create sales and generate income, they do not possess the knowledge of your intermediate objectives. And these are the early stage goals of any collaboration.

The curiosity of the potential collaborator as per your needs is understandable. They understand that for the collaboration to be fruitful for them, it would also have to be mutually fruitful for you. It is your responsibility to communicate your targeted results. These would probably not be direct sales, but rather results that would allow you to increase your sales, such as marketing benefits, client relation benefits and so on.

Suggest the Collaboration

If we go back to our example of the two baby instructors, we identified that both enter the collaboration for similar reasons; they both were looking to expand their market reach. Therefore, at this stage, each would detail why she needs to expand her market reach. She may reveal that she is new to this town, and therefore, although having a very good reputation in her previous location, she now needs to create new market awareness, all from the start. Therefore, her main need is for reputation-building support. Other needs may include gaining access to "warmer" audiences, thus saving on marketing costs, while the ability to present her service to people that are already trusting the collaborator's reputation, will shorten her sales process.

Being new to the area may result in other needs that could benefit the other party while deriving from this same collaboration. As a new teaching service, working with young mothers, there is a need for a studio or a gym. As the specific characteristics of baby teaching requires a safe environment, this physical need would, by definition, limit the availability of relevant rooms that the new instructor may locate as suitable for her needs. Thus, stating to her potential collaborator that she holds that need, may also assist her. That need for a physical location may become a major element of their collaboration, even though it was not considered earlier. She may share that she has yet to rent a studio.

At earlier stages, we talked about exploring the other party's needs, and we noted that they may not clearly share all their hopes and needs.

However, now, as she shares her need for studio space, the potential collaborator may just reveal that she does not utilize the full potential of her studio. We may learn that the other instructor is renting the studio for several days a week, each for half a day. However, her business activity does not utilize the full time she rents the space. The new need for a studio, as we just revealed, gives her the reason to disclose that she would be happy to offer the studio for a few hours at lower rental costs.

This unexpectedly becomes a new pillar in their collaboration. The initiator of the discussion was aiming to fulfill her marketing objectives, but now, as she has revealed her other needs and objectives, she has found a solution for her physical space-renting objective. The new connection between the two marketing collaborators will be a major pillar in their relationship. It would cause the local collaborator to drive more clients toward the newcomer; not only because of her interest in the earlier discussed collaboration's marketing benefits, but also because now she has an interest that the other instructor will succeed. Her success would mean that she will pay rental fees for longer hours and for a longer period, which will help cover some of the collaborator's monthly rental fees.

Detailing all your needs may act as a discussion trigger point for solutions that you may not have been aware of earlier.

Detail Your Partner's Winning Interests

Revealing your discussion partner's new needs, business objectives and personal goals, holds the power to shift the board game. Once you listen carefully to their aspirations, you hold the real gold, the real power for success. You may have collected their interests and objectives during your preliminary market research, and you may have heard them during the initial discussion when you specifically asked for these. You may also have revealed their objectives whilst sharing your objectives. In any case, by now you have an expanded vision of the other person's business objectives and probably their life goals as well.

On the other hand, your discussion partner does not hold the same picture you have in your mind. Therefore, as the leader of this collaboration, it is your task to share your collaboration vision, starting with the more important element, your discussion partner's interests.

Our young-mothers instructor should start with the newly revealed interest, as we can now assess that it is a high priority need for her collaborator, and then progress down the list. It would sound like this: "As I am a new business in this area, one of my objectives is to locate a relevant space for my groups. I now understand that we may join forces here. I can rent your studio if we get the scheduling right, which I believe could be great for both of us, and it will provide new income for your business and reduce your monthly overhead."

Note that when stating the other party's objectives, I also elaborated the result; not only saying I understand that this is your need, but also immediately providing the vision of the outcome. I immediately created the excitement, to be applied one by one, by going through all their relevant objectives and drawing the winning picture for each.

Going through their list of interests, I would continue: "Once my groups are running, you will come as my guest and share an example of your teaching with my clients. With my recommendation, they are likely to become your clients too. And even if they are not relevant as clients for you at this stage, they would become what we call a "warm" audience. So, there would be a high probability that they would share your service with their friends that are relevant clients for you at this time. Our mutual recommendations will assist your marketing efforts, and save some of your advertisement costs." The aim of this practice is to energize the discussion and bring the other person's objective fulfillment interest to the front. Remember, we did not yet talk about money... that is intentional. We are on a mission to focus on the interests rather than on the position.

If we take the same approach as our used car example, we would detail the seller's interests as follows: "I understand your interest for selling this car is to cover a loan, or toward covering your daughter's wedding. I am sure you can get the best market price as relevant for current market behavior, as we saw in the Manheim Used Vehicle Value Index, allowing you to return to the wedding preparations as soon as possible." Again, we immediately provided the vision of the outcome; that is, that he may forget this sale hustle and return to the wedding preparations.

I hope by now you can feel the winds shifting. We took the simple sale process of "let's get the highest price for the car," and changed it to a new state of mind: "I am aware of market value, and it is even more important for me to get back to the wedding preparations, or to minimize my loan size as soon as possible." Talking about the interest is the key to concluding any negotiation with a WIN/WIN outcome. That is why it is also called interest-based negotiating. Talking about the interests is fundamental for reaching a successful collaboration.

Set the Full WIN/WIN Picture

We started by sharing our approach that we assume the other person is skilled in his profession and came ready with market knowledge. That means that we are aware that they do not believe in miracles. We understand that they do not think we just came to solve their business objectives because we are nice people. We know that they are waiting to hear what we want them to do for us.

Suggest the Collaboration

We have managed to get them excited that we are the right people to assist them in fulfilling their objectives and missions. But they are waiting to understand what may be demanded from them in return. Before we get into the tactical details of the collaboration, it is now time to complete the drawing of the collaboration WIN/WIN picture.

Going back to our young-mothers instructors, it would sound like: "Our full collaboration would mean that you will visit my groups and I will visit your groups. We would both provide each other with credibility. I would be able to start collecting clients for my groups faster and at no marketing costs, while being able to share my existing client lists that may order your online course, even though they are not local. My previous clients may also pass your message on to their friends that are local, as they trust my recommendation. I may also be renting your studio for several hours a week, for a good price, helping you reduce your monthly overhead."

In some cases, the WIN/WIN picture may be more complicated, making the collaborators' relationship even tighter, like in the real-life collaboration where I was helping that specific young-moms' instructor. The more complex the collaboration, the higher the importance is to draw the full collaboration picture for all participants, before trying to conclude the deal.

In that case, my client was teaching infant movement classes. She was moving her business to a new town and was looking for a studio that had mattresses and would be safe for babies. She did locate two such studios, but renting a studio at an hourly market price was too much for a new business with no local clients.

The next step was to observe these two studios and see if any of them had needs that were obvious enough that they could be used to open a discussion based on interests. We have learned that one of the two was working with children, thus using the studio only during the afternoons after the kids were home from school. Our instructor was working with young mothers on maternity leave, meaning they were looking for morning activities.

This was our base for planning the collaboration. During the discussions, we revealed that our discussion partner was a person eager to reduce overhead, while the main focus was on managing the business and not on spending time looking to sub-lease the studio. That understanding opened the ground for a more elaborated collaboration. We could offer that the instructor will eventually rent all the mornings, at a price that would cover a substantial cost of the rental agreement.

She would invest the time and offer the studio to other relevant instructors as well. The triangle collaboration would mean that the main leaseholder would eventually cover seventy percent of the overall rental costs, and not have to deal with any of the businesses renting from him, other than one, which is a big WIN for him.

The new instructors, sub-renting from my client, would be renting for only a few hours a week, but they would be charged a very low rate compared to the going market rate, meaning they also get a WIN. They also get to present their service within their groups if relevant, so they also get a marketing WIN, leading them toward using the studio for longer hours.

Now, what interests does my client, our leading collaborator, fulfill? Offering such a deal to the prime rental holder, led him to shift from asking for an hourly charge, to a lower charge, due to a half-a-day monthly agreement. That translates to a much lower cost per hour. He also understood that it would take my client time to fill her groups, and a longer time to bring in new instructors.

Suggest the Collaboration

For that, he was willing to provide her with a free pass to his facility for the first three months, and during the following three months to pay only for her proportionate use. That by itself was a big WIN for her, but then we continue. Her goal was to work with only 3–4 groups a week, meaning she had the place empty for some 15 hours a week, during the mornings. The new instructors sub-renting from her were glad to pay reduced hourly costs. But they were still being charged in relation to the higher hourly going rate, and for her that meant that once they took the full 15 hours, they would overpay her rental fees, leaving her with a new marketing budget, so that was a second WIN for her.

To continue, as the studio was set up for children's safety, we could assume that most instructors that would arrive, would have children-based businesses, which means that their clients may also have young siblings at home, and their mothers would be potential clients for her too. So, presenting her business toward her sub-rental clients, would save her on marketing costs and provide her with their trust for free, another big WIN. And obviously, the main leaseholder would be happy to allow her to approach his clients too.

You can see that the more complicated collaboration, once reached, leads to very strong dependency between the collaborators. The main leaseholder has a high interest that she would succeed in her endeavor, so her overhead would remain low forever. Her sub-leasers would be happy to pay low rental fees, saving them money and allowing them to grow their businesses, thus using the studio for longer hours. As these two corners of the triangle get closer to their goals, they provide our instructor, my client, with a great start along her business path, and provide the safety that such a collaboration would last longer.

Chapter 8

Close the Deal

"Risk comes from not knowing what you're doing."
— Warren Buffett

Introduce the New Board Game

Arriving successfully at the final stage implies that both of the potential collaborators are happy with what they have learned of each other, and have a positive sense of the future. Hence, we need to finalize the deal. In a sale of product negotiation, this is the stage where we talk about the product value, complete the negotiation and finalize the deal.

In our vehicle sale example, the buyer, who is the one leading the WIN/WIN strategy, will now collect all the data and present his conclusion. That would sound something like this: "My friend, let us gather all the issues raised and finalize the deal. We have talked about your need to get the best market price as soon as possible so that you may return the loan. I am also interested in finalizing this car purchase project as soon as possible. We have looked at the Manheim Used Vehicle Value Index and have learned that the car's index value is just over $15,000. We also agreed that the physical condition is such-and-such, and we got professional advice that the mechanical condition is such-and-such. Do you agree?"

You start with gathering and presenting all the information that was already agreed; so the only response you should receive is a confirmation that you have a similar understanding of the board game. Now, before hassling the price, you need to make sure that your negotiation partner does not change position and increase the asking price. So, you continue: "At the beginning, we agreed that both of us are looking for the best achievable market price, and we both respect each other to know the market trends. Taking all that into account while being aware that the market is a little slow now, I think we can also agree that getting the index price tag is impossible. So, as the index price is …, I would like to offer …. "

In presenting your case, using the WIN/WIN negotiation technique, you have managed to shift the party's passions from what we saw in Chapter 5—when Joe was planning to ask for $18,000, while David was aiming to offer $9,500—to a much smaller gap. If that hadn't happened, it is highly likely that no deal could have been achieved. However, both have now agreed that the price should be somewhere below the $15,000 index price. So, real negotiation would probably be between $16,000 and $12,000. Now, that is achievable. The needle will stabilize in accordance with the personal relations created. At that stage, both have some sense of who would go the extra mile toward concluding the deal, and the deal will finalize itself at the best value for both.

We have concluded the interest-based negotiation technique for sales of products and services. However, our interest is to utilize the same technique for the setting of a business collaboration; therefore, the following adjustments may be required.

At this stage, both are aware of the interests presented by the other person. They have two unrelated interest lists, and there is a need to clear the board. As you are probably the leader of this discussion, your role would be to set the board game.

Setting the board game is the most important stage in the process, as this would be the first time both parties can look at the full picture and make a conscious decision that they wish to participate in that specific collaboration.

The board game would include only the relevant interests of both parties, only those interests that could be addressed by the activities of the other person and the collaboration at large.

In the process, you have learned that some of your business interests could not be fulfilled by that potential collaborator for a variety of reasons. All these interests are to be removed at this stage.

The board game presentation will start with detailing the interests of the other person. You mention their interests as they have presented them, and elaborate why and how they would be fulfilled via the collaboration. Only then do you spotlight yourself and detail which of your interests would be fulfilled via this collaboration, while concluding with your bigger goals and how this collaboration would assist you in getting closer to your bigger goals. Obviously, it's best if you can also elaborate how this collaboration would get your partner closer to their bigger goals.

Once there is an agreement that fulfilling these goals is important to both collaborators, we dig into the details, making sure both see the details in the same way.

Roles, Tasks and Responsibilities

A collaboration is a joint, choreographed dance. Imagine one dancer jumping and expecting the other to catch them and lift them up, while the other dancer just makes a turn and smiles at the audience. You would not like to be either dancer at that moment.

Both collaborators have just agreed that they see the board game the same way, and they both wish to proceed and gain the benefits of working together. Earlier in this book, we described the collaboration as a soft agreement when compared with the detailed legal agreement required when setting up a registered partnership or a joint venture. However, in any scenario when two or more entities collaborate, there is a basic need to make sure all are aligned.

In the following pages, we will touch base on the main collaboration tactical understandings as required for a successful, long-lasting relationship, starting with roles, tasks and responsibilities.

Collaboration realization is aimed at co-operation that takes advantage of the relative advantages each collaborator brings to the table, and is aimed at achieving defined goals. Here, the partners establish organizational structures and processes related to the responsibility for carrying out tasks. They define the conditions that require coordination, and they define the authority to make decisions. The transition from the announcement and goodwill phase, to the action phase, requires a higher level of commitment. The partners are exposed in their weakness, and identify new capabilities in themselves and their partners. The collaboration implementation phase requires improved communication channels, which require to be maintained constantly throughout.

For example, a low level of trust and commitment is required for the decision to publish a recommendation for the other party's business, as one party shares with his audience and followers the other party's marketi-ng event. In that example, you have no responsibility for their service, but only for inviting people to their marketing event, where each client will have to make their own conscious decision. However, a higher level of trust is required when you may be asked to revert your audience toward ordering your collaborator's products or services directly. Note that this is a two-way path: Once one collaborator shows a high trust level, the other will reciprocate.

In setting the responsibilities, the discussion should be conducted at two levels. One level is the client's path. Walk the process through the client's eyes and make sure you determine who is responsible for each step. The second level is the background logistics. There is a requirement to specify exactly who does what and why.

For example, a marketing collaboration aimed at bringing paying clients to one collaborator, while strengthening the other person's brand and exposure, may include setting a joint marketing event as a starting point for meeting new clients. Therefore, in relation to the client experience level, there is a need to decide whose name is on top, who is making the introduction speech, etc. At the background level, there is a need to decide who would book the venue, who would take care of the technical issues like computing and audio elements, who would take care of the refreshments, who would talk to the press and who is responsible for the social media planning and exposure.

In a well-planned collaboration, a great part of the operation could be based on pre-owned capabilities. Each collaborator would bring their best abilities and, together, they would be able to progress. Although there will be elements that would inevitably require financial investment, now is the time to specify and elaborate how much money is assessed to be required, why it is required, who makes the investment and why this collaborator is responsible for that investment.

When drafting a partnership agreement, the role of this collaboration is part of the risk management. The legal consultant's aim would be to minimize disagreement and the risk of legal actions. When setting a collaboration, the aim of the parties is different, so the risk of legal suits is minimal—if things do not work well, the collaboration would just melt away. The aim for detailing the roles and responsibilities focuses on greasing the wheels of the collaboration cart. The better the wheels are greased, the smoother the ride will be. The main purpose is to get to the aimed result as fast as possible, and a clear action-item list will get both collaborators fulfilling their joint objectives more quickly, and closer to the revenue.

The Revenue Model

A business plan is divided into several elements. The chapters relating to the business economics will include the operations model, which will detail how the business spends on operations, while the revenue model will specify how the business makes money. The revenue model will detail the earning strategy. It would include the products' costs and their respective sales price, and any other earning models as relevant for the business.

A collaboration's revenue model will have a different appearance, and may include a more complicated revenue structure. Note that this may imply a longer acceptance process by both parties. A simple revenue model states that the product cost is "X," while the markup is 15%, leading to a profit of "Y." The collaboration may include revenue that is not money. However, it should still be measurable.

Earlier, each collaborator specified their intended gains from this collaboration. These may have included direct sales, but most likely also included marketing gains or saving on manpower cost.

The collaboration revenue model will include all revenues, and the aim of this stage is to reach an agreement and an understanding that these are feasible and achievable.

Using our earlier example of the infant-movement instructor, who contracted a lease for a studio from a business that is focused on afternoon classes, they have set a relationship where the leaseholder would benefit by having peace of mind while generating continuous income (i.e. reducing his overhead). He would also benefit from a mutual client referral system, both from that instructor and from her sub-leasers. In return, he was happy to grant three months of free access, and further periods of relative payment per use. The role and responsibility accepted by my client, the infant-movement instructor, was to take care of marketing and setting a mutual referral system. The revenue model of such a collaboration would detail not only the studio costs but mainly the marketing benefits. A clear nominal amount of referrals is best specified. Although both are aware that this is only an estimation, they both rely on these estimations when reverting to their business plans and exploring how far they are progressing toward achieving their goals. In our case, they would specify that the infant-movement instructor is aiming to use the place for three groups within a four-month period. She would bring in two to three other sub-leasers. Overall, there is an expectation that 200 families would become morning customers of that studio, while all would be exposed to the main leaseholder's business that takes place during the afternoons.

For the main leaseholder, that exposure is a marketing revenue. His marketing gain is twofold by saving on marketing expenses and sales efforts. Only when he is able to account for these revenue benefits, he would agree to provide the movement instructor with savings on her lease agreement.

In cases where two businesses collaborate for marketing purposes, we can expect that one of them would be closer to the money (i.e. their sales process will benefit faster from that collaboration). The collaboration's revenue model would have to account for that too.

Therefore, in the case that one business exposes the other business's service to their clients, with the main intention of bettering their clients, the referring business revenue is marketing revenue, and their clients are glad to hear they are thinking of them and, in the future, are more likely to re-use their service again.

However, the referred business revenue is twofold. First, they save on marketing expenses, and then they gain new clients and new sales. The collaboration's revenue has to account for that inequality. Therefore, the business that is gaining the immediate clients will have to add some referral fee to the other party, thus unifying the collaboration revenue model. Both would gain marketing revenues and immediate fiscal revenue—one from sales and the other by a form of referral commission. The referral commission by itself is not strong enough to justify the collaboration for the long run, but the marketing revenues are.

Time Frame for Success

The collaboration strategy holds a lifeline for any small business, reducing marketing costs and shortening sales processes. Once the interest-based negotiating tool becomes part of the annual business plan, an income expectation is created. In a large organization, the marketing VP will set the collaboration, and once all is agreed, the fulfillment responsibility shall be passed to the sales VP, who will designate one of the sales teams to manage the progress of the sales.

In a small business, there would usually be only one person who is responsible for the collaboration progress, from its conception stage until the proceeds are visible in the business's bank account. A project agreement would include a specific appendix or a supplement detailing the project's timetable. As we discussed earlier, the collaboration is a softer partnership model; however, agreeing on the timetable is nevertheless important.

The time frame or scheduling supplement outlines the expected product deliveries and the expected progress along the project's stages, and it details the payment schedule in accordance with the deliveries. Most agreements specify a fixed end date, but some state that deliveries will continue until one or both parties wish to cancel the agreement. The collaboration is a more complicated project, however; unless the timetable is clear and agreed by both collaborators, nothing will happen in real life, and nothing will be visible in the business's bank account.

I have seen many small businesses be proud of nice collaborations they have established, only to discover, a year later, that they have received no income following that collaboration. When investigating such cases, I usually discover that one person was waiting for the other person to take the first action, while the second person was not aware that due to his lack of activity, the whole collaboration fell apart. Preventing such a catastrophe is usually simple.

Reaching an agreed collaboration time frame is a simple task. However, when ignored, the whole collaboration disappears. The main advantage of reaching a WIN/WIN collaboration agreement is that both people are enthusiastic of their joint potential. Therefore, now is the best time to set the time frame for success.

It is recommended to set a different meeting, where you discuss the collaboration schedule. Give yourself a few days to consider all the advantages you may gain from the finalized collaboration as was agreed. Consider the action items that you would need to deliver, and those of the other person. Ponder on the details, and write which tasks may require greater attention by any of you.

The next meeting should be dedicated to addressing the tasks of each party, and figuring out together how long and how complicated each task may be. The outcome of this meeting should be a list of action items and tasks, and the relevant time frame for each task. Note that a collaboration is like a chess match, though not as opposing sides. Each player has to consider the actions taken by the other person and respond. Therefore, in many cases, the task scheduling would zigzag between both collaborators.

In any case, at any point of time, you need to be able to revert back to the agreed timetable and see where you stand. The collaboration schedule plan is the tool to be used for an ongoing assessment, whether you are progressing along the way or have diverted unconsciously.

A weekly comparison between the collaboration planned schedule and the reality of the business will provide both collaborators with greater chances of staying on track. The examination of the agreed time frame will also serve as a relationship maintenance tool, as it will reduce the misunderstandings, thus increasing the collaboration's success potential.

Technicalities for Success

Once the collaboration timeline is set, the real work will start. Until now, we have elaborated on getting the two businesses aligned toward joining forces. Being happy that both have decided to collaborate is not the final goal. The final goal is to progress both business's interests. Thus, the relationship must connect to a timeline and a list of mini tasks. These tasks are the real lifeline of the collaboration. You may have high expectations, and the relationship with the other collaborator may be great, but if both of the collaborators fail to take action, then nothing will progress.

"God is in the details." Every business specializes in different activities that derive from the service they offer and the market they are customarily serving. An efficient organization will correlate its activities and marketing goals to perfection. In perfecting the collaboration, both participants will have to specify who does what and why, taking into account the strengths and weaknesses of both.

Here is a guideline of different technical aspects that are to be addressed:

Marketing – Marketing is the backbone of sales. The collaboration marketing will include the branding of the joint venture, where relevant. Dictate which marketing activities are required in order to brand the new collaboration in front of the relevant audience. Marketing will also include the market research and the product or service launching. Provide the required materials, in text format, video and social media exposure, leading toward making the sales processes work smoothly. In any case, the coordination between the collaborators, as per the marketing of their new entity, is crucial, while the ultimate aim of the marketing activities is to increase revenue for both collaborators.

Sales – Sales are the revenue generating activities in any organization. It is important that the collaboration be focused on sales activities so as to provide the long-term interest for its survival. In a collaboration that is a dual-head activity, it is wise to conduct an open discussion and identify who holds the better sales staff; and if needed, then maybe join a third party that would accept the sales responsibility. Part of the collaboration may include one party educating the other on sale techniques, or on client-service practices and so on.

The aim of the sales team is to convert the collaborators' client database and new leads into paying customers, while providing feedback to the marketing team in relation to the efficacy of their activities.

Customer service – The product sold or the service offered by the collaboration may mainly derive from one of the collaborators. However, the clients see both collaborators as one. Therefore, the customer service would benefit both businesses, even if there were a need for technical support just for a specific product. The customer satisfaction is the main accomplishment that both collaborators may utilize in the future. Good customer service holds the power to bring back lost customers and turn them into paying clients. A simple CRM system is a great tool for any business size, thus the social media may also be used as an open communication channel with your clients.

Supply chain – My experience with small businesses reveals that this is the most neglected element in all their business activities. Having the best product or service is not enough. It has to be delivered to the client in the most efficient manner, relating to each market segment and niche. Consider an e-commerce supply as a simple example, where you aim for the product to arrive to the client at the earliest time, or in an acceptable time frame, packed nicely and with the relevant shipping documentation attached. The same applies to any service. You may be delivering a service in your office or clinic, where the packaging may not include a boxed item but a service that is "packaging" elements, such as the atmosphere you create in the room. The service provided in your clinic does not include attaching documentation similar to a shipped item, but it does include offering a drink in the waiting room, providing relevant marketing brochures, etc.

The collaboration supply chain is the sum of activities that ensures the client receives the joint service at the highest satisfaction rate.

Budgeting – Any business activity requires a budget, even if a set collaboration does not require a financial investment. The time dedicated is budgeted activity. Expressing the budgeted elements during the collaboration structuring is important for both collaborators. Any activity performed must be both appreciated as an investment by the non-active collaborator, and assessed wisely by the active collaborator. This may be sales effort, marketing activity, the value of the facility that is granted toward the collaboration and so on.

The budget helps determine the value of the collaboration for each collaborator. Proper planning would be reviewed by the scope of budget utilized during the collaboration performance, while serving as a comparison tool for the assessment, whether the collaboration has achieved higher success rates compared to your last year's marketing efforts.

Accounting – In a collaboration, the accounting phase is a separate topic for discussion. While any business is bound by accountancy regulations and proper invoicing, the collaboration will include internal profit sharing. One would usually invoice the clients, and the other would internally invoice for their part. Thus, these elements have to be discussed and agreed. Does the relevant internal payment pass between the collaborators per each sale? On a monthly/quarterly basis? Note that the collaborators would usually come from different market niches. That is the main reason for their collaboration. However, that may entail different accounting practices. One may come from a real estate market, where each transaction is of high value and takes time; while the other could come from an online marketing niche, where transactions are of low value, but the business serves a great number of clients each day. For our discussion purposes, one would consider payment per transaction or sale as normal, while the other may consider weekly or even quarterly payment as normal.

Reaching an accounting understanding and a unilateral language is key for better communication throughout.

Auditing – Finally, yet importantly, any business activity must include an auditing system. Collecting money and high sales is a nice business goal. However, there is a need to determine if the collaboration is performing its role in the best way possible. Auditing is a way to check if the clients' responses are in the expected or sought after satisfaction rate. It is comparing all activities with the relevant guidelines as agreed upon when setting the collaboration to work. It is necessary that all the activities are monitored and audited. Detailing the auditing manner is the final activity that would make sure both collaborators feel safe to embark on their joint endeavor.

Risks, Concerns and Opportunities

Any time a business embarks on a new venture, it should be expected that some new risks would follow. As we are progressing toward a dual (or more) business collaboration, the exposure to new risks is true and relevant for all parties concerned. Therefore, an open discussion must take place. The expected interaction would be that the person approached for the collaboration will raise more concerns, since the approaching person may have considered some risk exposure and has decided he is okay to proceed with the collaboration building. However, that is not the full truth. During their collaboration discussion, as detailed in earlier chapters, both parties have learned new information relating to the other person's intentions, beliefs and mode of doing business. Thus, both need to openly discuss what their concerns are and what risks they are able to identify, while utilizing their joint abilities to minimize the risk factors.

The Harvard Business Review identifies three risk categories, and with some adoptions, these could serve us in examining the new collaboration proposition.

Preventable risks – These are internal risks arising from within the organization, which are controllable and ought to be eliminated or avoided. This mainly refers to actions taken for a short-term benefit while crossing the red lines. It is taking an unethical or even an illegal action for a short-term benefit. For example, illegal use of a client database, or making a bold, untrue marketing statement aimed at increasing sales, and so on.

These types of risks are best managed by active prevention measures. In the collaboration setting, you have an interest that the other party's salesperson does not over-sell your ability while jeopardizing your reputation. Once you identify such a risk, be it from the potential activity of any of the collaborator's personnel, it is best to pre-set the business norms and practices both should follow.

Strategy risks (or "no pain no gain") – Any business endeavor incorporates some risk. These risks are accepted after careful consideration. The development of a new drug is a very costly endeavor with no pre-knowledge that all the efforts and investment will bear fruits. However, the economic potential is so great that the risks are acceptable.

The strategic risks cannot be avoided, as they are the other side of the same coin of profit. Instead, both collaborators need to set a risk-management system intended to reduce the chances of these risks materializing or getting out of control. Setting a risk-management system is the wise tool that allows a business to take calculated risks while actively controlling them, or controlling the risk-events from harming the business.

Joining in a collaboration exposes the business to a new variety of strategic risks. We expect any businessperson to be aware of the strategic risks of their trade. However, joining a collaboration may expose the business to risks that are out of his normal business practices. That does not mean these are dangerous risks that must be avoided. The collaborator may operate in a different business sphere, and that is exactly your collaboration potential. Their different activity means that they are normally exposed to risks that you are not familiar with, and thus you have never set procedures to avoid or control these risks.

The collaboration discussion intention is to reveal what risks are new to any of the parties, and how each may assist the other in controlling these risks for the benefit of the joint collaboration.

External risks – These are risks that are out of our control, like earthquakes, a worldwide epidemic or political changes. There is very little a business can do to control its exposure to such risks, other than buying a relevant insurance policy. Research shows that people are discouraged from considering or taking relevant protection measurements until it is too late.

When describing the inseparable risk elements of war, thus relevant just the same for doing business, President Harry S. Truman is quoted as saying, "If you cannot stand the heat, get out of the kitchen," which means that any business opportunity comes with a risk factor attached. All that a businessperson has to assess is that the opportunity is greater than the attached risk.

In Chapter 2, we noted the abundance of opportunities that will be revealed once collaboration becomes an active business tool. Acknowledging that requires that you develop or embrace an opportunity assessment procedure that resonates with your personality and business views.

A market opportunity assessment needs to be tailored to the specific industry and circumstances, and will include the mixture of the following:

Market assessment – This relates to the quantification of the market and your potential revenue that this opportunity brings. A suggested assessment procedure would be to respond to the following questions:

- What is the market demand for the product, be it in value ($) or in volume (product units)?
- What is your current reach toward that market?
- How much do you need to invest in growing your market exposure?
- What is your realistic potential market capture in a year or three years' time?
- Do you understand the specific market behavior? Can you assess the market trends and where the market will be in the next 3–5 years?
- Can you create a business model while considering the market behavior?

Risk assessment – Consider what short-term and long-term risks you are able to identify at the initiation stage. Then consider if you are able to construct some risk mitigation strategy, or business resilience procedures.

Growth assessment – After you are convinced that the opportunity presented is likely to open new market horizons for your business, and with a manageable risk, then comes the deeper market exploration stage. Here is a list of questions that should assist in assessing the growth opportunity:

- Who are the competitors, and how would you differentiate your product or service from theirs?

- Create customer "avatar"/"ideal customer personas," and explore their satisfaction from current marketed products or services.

- What marketing channels are relevant for achieving best ROI (return on investment) for that specific product or service?
- How complicated is it to achieve an initial client database?

As our aim is to assess collaboration opportunities, we automatically gain the united collaborated force for solving each of these questions.

Set Higher Future Joint Success

Last but not least is the joint goal setting for the new collaboration. Just like your business is energized by your higher goals, so is the collaboration. When setting the collaborated activity's goals, we need to start by understanding the other person's limitations. Understanding their limitations or areas where they would rather not be involved, would serve as an expectation gauge. The collaborator's limitations may set the line, beyond which there would be a need to recruit external help or have a third party join the collaboration.

Once the limitations are addressed, you are free to highlight the strengths of both collaborators. See where one plus one equals three. Make sure you dedicate enough time to recognize your partner's strengths. Some of their strengths are probably the reason why you have approached them in the first place. However, now it is time to recognize all their other strengths too, as these would play a key role in your joint success. While each collaborator focuses on the other person's strengths, both fuel each other's motivation to grow and expand.

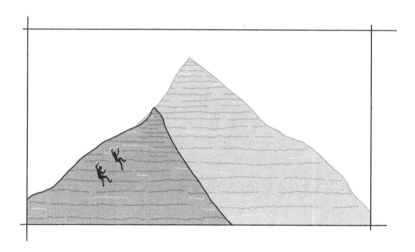

As joint motivation is created, it is a good idea to immediately set even higher goals. Explore what opportunities may open in the future, following the collaboration success. It may be that two businesses have embarked on a marketing collaboration. Their initial objective is specific. Nevertheless, they can create a joint vision. Their future vision will state that once this collaboration is successful, they would duplicate the success once every two or three months. Suddenly, the marketing opportunity that drove the collaboration becomes a sustainable business model and a recurring marketing activity that may derive revenue, not as a single activity but as a long-term revenue provider.

The long-term success model possesses the motivational power to solve any difficulties that may emerge along the way. This is the reverse approach from the business modeling we learned at the start of our joint adventure. At the start of this book, we identified that in order to achieve success, any business has to start with setting its own higher goals. Once these are set, we learned how to plan our business path, including the setting of intermediate missions and objectives. The collaboration is a result of our wish to fulfill our objectives. Therefore, the success of the collaboration would be measured against our predetermined objectives.

Now I direct you toward creating your own opportunities, giving you the power to shatter the glass ceiling. You have created a successful collaboration. You have managed to unite two businesses for their respective benefits and their respective mission fulfillments. Why stop there? Why not use that joint success to fulfill higher goals?

The comparison of this exercise to your business plan is the same as the ratio between your annual goal and your ten-year goal. The current collaboration is the annual goal, while your future high potential opportunity is compared with the ten-year business goal.

I am urging you to set new, higher goals for this collaboration, even before you have made the first step. Invest the time to jointly imagine higher goals. That future may include having other businesses join your collaboration, or approaching new markets together, or anything that would get you excited—excited enough to fuel your motivation to embark on your collaboration with great force.

Chapter 9

The Networking Way to Clients

"In business, it's about people. It's about relationships."
– Kathy Ireland

Stop Spreading Business Cards

During a conference coffee break, you join a hundred of your peers and clients. You have been invited to a conference as an executive or a salesperson. Maybe you joined a networking event as an independent business owner. You enter the hall, and fifteen potential clients immediately rush toward you and ask for your service… do you recall such an experience?

I am sure you do not; that never happens. It is more likely that before entering the hall, you make a wish to attract at least one good client. Then you enter the hall and see lots of unfamiliar faces. You may have located one friend in the audience, and both of you take your coffee to a side table. Occasionally, that friend will introduce you to some of their friends, and you will hand out a few of your nice business cards, displaying a forced smile and feeling that you pushed the business cards because you know that this is the right thing to do. You are not alone; we all feel the same.

In a study, people were asked what they were feeling when approaching another person for the purpose of making a new business introduction. The participants reported that they felt an urge for cleaning. In simple words, networking makes us feel dirty. Sound familiar?

The purpose of this chapter is to open your mind and enrich your bank account. This short chapter will reveal why networking did not work for you until today, and what you should do from now on to attract real income out of a conference or a networking event.

The common networking practice today is to ask each participant for a short self-presentation, with the general perception that the relevant clients are present in the room. However, in reality, that is not the case. Independent business owners join networking groups and meet the same crowd throughout the year. Executives visit industry events and meet their peers. The social activity during these events is the main activity that really takes place, and business cards are handed out as a secondary activity.

At this stage of the book, you are already aware that building collaborations is one of your strongest business tools. Therefore, at this stage, we would consider the networking event as a platform for setting fruitful collaborations.

You are invited to discover 36 more places where you can locate potential collaborators, at www.CollaborateSuccess.com.

With that approach in mind, we stop looking for clients at networking events. We stop handing out business cards. We change the disk, make the right preparations and turn these events into income generators.

Explore Your Business Inner-Self

First things first, before leaving the comfort of your home or office, there is a need to clearly declare what the purpose of your business is, and who your ideal clients are.

Why is this so important? In the past, there has been a lot of talk about target audiences, and if your business has already been operating for few years, I can imagine that you have developed products and services aimed at different people with different needs; and in short, you are now aiming at a number of different target audiences.

All is well if you are happy with your business's standing and if you have no desire to leap forward, and no urge to set a new course for your business and life achievements.

Therefore, it is critical to stop, look inside, forget everything you are doing for a moment and plan a new business path. The first step is to stop talking to the audience and start talking to your ideal customer directly. In today's market, people are bombarded with advertisements; thus, we have all developed automatic blocks, providing us with a notion and feeling of control. Thus, your clients are also blocking your publications. The only way to cross that barrier is to approach the ideal customer directly. They will feel the connection; the barrier would be lowered, and the sale may proceed.

Note that you have three seconds to grab their attention. Within these three seconds, we all make the decision whether to invest any attention or move elsewhere. As that is the case, I recommend you focus on those clients that you are happy to serve. Focus only on one product and one client at a time. Obviously, there is no need to reject other clients when they come; however, focus the marketing efforts on your ideal client. The ideal customer is the one that you are happy to serve, for whom your service solves a major problem he/she is facing, and whom is able to pay for your product or service.

Your ability to understand your ideal customer will allow you to grab the customer's attention. Once they become aware that you identify with their pain and feel that you are able to solve their problem, they will invest further time to explore your service or product.

However, as we discussed, your clients are not visiting these networking events. Our purpose during that event is to locate the relevant collaborator that would send our ideal customers toward our business. Therefore, the first mission is to make a conscious decision as to who the one client is that we would rather serve, and what our best product is for that client.

The same consideration that applies to focusing on a singular ideal customer, also applies to focusing on a single product or service. The singular focus you develop is a powerful marketing behavior; it would expose your enthusiasm in serving that specific person. And in a networking event where everyone is searching for clients, your enthusiasm is much more important than your business card.

In the following pages, we shall reveal how that enthusiasm serves as a collaboration magnet.

Understand Your Client's Surrounding

A significant part of the avatar/ideal customer research you have conducted will reveal where the ideal customer is hanging out. You will need to target your marketing efforts to these exact locations. These are also the locations where you would locate the best collaboration opportunities.

It is possible that these are physical places, such as a sports club, community center, university, regional industrial area, etc. You may also identify online locations, such as forums, social media communities and certain media channels where your ideal customer acquires their news and professional information, and so on.

Note that some of the avatar research has led you to insights relating to the purchase decision-maker identity. For example, regarding a couple therapy service, the one who usually closes the deal is the woman, even though both partners come voluntarily to these consultation meetings. So, you need to focus your marketing efforts in a feminine form. However, a parallel, different campaign for men can strengthen the bond with the client and speed up the process of the couple making a purchase decision.

If it is a product for children, then the parent is the one who makes the decision. However, it would be a good idea to set a double marketing campaign, targeting both the parent and the child in parallel.

Further information you have discovered while walking in your ideal customer's shoes, would be the identity of other service providers they are using. Once you consider your client as a person and not as a target market, you notice that they have other needs that appear to be irrelevant for your marketing activity. However, these separate needs could serve your business as an open entrance point toward your clients. The other service providers, those that solve your ideal client's other needs, are your best potential collaborators.

For example, a youth sport instructor may discover that their ideal clients, who are girls 15 to 18 years of age, are attending local youth movement meetings. They attend a specific school, and their parents are attending some communal groups.

If you are a mortgage consultant, your clients are using, or have used in the past, the services of a law office or a real estate agent.

Using the collaboration glasses, it is clear that these professionals are not our competitors. These other service providers are serving our targeted clients for their other needs. Reverting to our earlier infant-movement instructor and the babies sleep instructor, we have identified that both serve the same mothers. They both serve the same clients for their different family needs. The collaboration between these two has saved both businesses on marketing investments, while both have benefited from higher client perception. Each has gained client trust by utilizing the trust already granted to the respective collaborator.

For locating the best collaborators, there is a need to respond to the following questions:

- Whom are the service providers serving my ideal client?
- Where are the physical locations that the ideal customer and/or their suppliers are hanging out at?
- To what population segment does my ideal customer belong? Within that population, the referrals will be passed on.

In short, the best collaborations would evolve between two service or product providers that are serving the same market segments but are in no competition.

Set Your Networking Mission

We have already established that the ideal customer is probably not attending our networking events. The implication is that our networking mission has just changed. No longer are we to search for clients at these events; there is no reason to spread business cards as the receiving person will probably forget the card two minutes after they received it. The main mission during the networking event is to locate the specific service or product provider that serves the ideal client, the avatar.

A business offering cosmetic products may consider all people as their potential clients. But the investment in identifying a specific avatar would reveal that they are looking for women of a specific age group. During a networking event, they may locate one or two of these ideal clients; however, if they locate a hair designer specializing in that age group, that hair designer is able to send their ideal customers toward them on a daily basis.

An attorney specializing in land law would have slim chances of locating homebuyers/sellers in that networking event. Spreading business cards will not lead to any incoming business. However, it is possible to locate mortgage consultants and real estate agents at these events. Setting collaborations with these service providers may point clients toward the attorney on a regular basis.

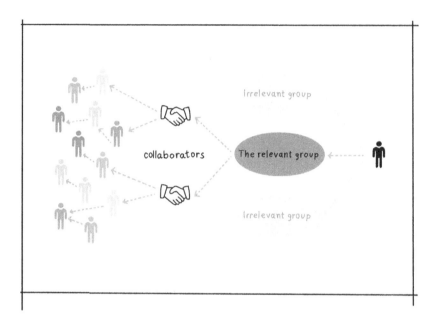

The networking mission is therefore to identify one or two specific people that may become collaborators as they serve the same clients. The networking mission is to locate such a person and open a direct discussion on how you may help each other. Make the right presentation that would lead toward further meetings where you would set the collaboration.

I hope something has changed for you while reading these lines, and that some new ideas just pop out.

The cosmetic products provider should stop wasting time approaching all women in the audience and spreading brochures and samples. The coffee break at the event can be used to approach one or two hair designers, setting the ground so that they would later establish a direct road from their business to yours.

While setting the networking mission, the following questions need to be asked:

- What do I want to achieve during that networking event? Direct clients/referrals/self-branding?
- Who is the "person" I wish to locate? Specify at least three different professionals that serve your ideal customer for their different needs.

Prepare your pitch. The networking pitch does not offer your product's benefits. It focuses on the reasons why that person should collaborate with you, as we will discuss in the following pages.

Only after these preparatory steps are taken is it relevant to step forward and join a networking event.

Locate the Right Networking Group

As always, preparation leads to success. The better prepared you are, the better the results achieved. Once the potential collaborators have been identified, it is possible to locate them. If the cosmetics supplier has identified that their potential collaborators are hair designers, then there is no sense in joining a networking group of real estate agents.

In recent years, networking has become a business buzz word. The abundance of networking events can spin any person's mind. Wherever we look and at any given time, it is possible to identify several opportunities for networking events. These are organized by industrial or professional organizations, local authorities, small-business organizations, and organizations specializing in setting up networking groups. The wealth of networking opportunities hides the risk of not seeing the forest for the trees.

A side comment for small business owners: The networking groups provide further advantages that are not the focus of this book; nevertheless, they are of great value. An independent employee working alone from home, or an owner of a small business employing several employees, may feel lonesome. They work alone, or feel alone amongst their employees. The networking event provides an opportunity to mingle with their peers, and an opportunity to break the isolation. An independent employee is missing the office coffee or cigarette breaks. The networking event may fulfill that void. Setting a networking mission as a mingling opportunity is just as important. One of the independent business owner's high goals will always be to keep their motivation high, and mingling with their peers is a key tool for achieving that goal. Utilizing the networking event for the purpose of keeping spirits high is important. Though it is not the purpose of this book, it is a valid goal, and if you so decide, then I urge you to clearly note for yourself that this is your networking goal, thus not becoming frustrated from not getting new clients at these events.

Earlier, we identified and targeted the relevant professionals that we wish to meet for the purpose of setting our collaborations. Now we need to identify where they are networking. Here are a list of preparatory steps that would get you closer to these people, and make your networking efforts pay off.

- Collect a list of all networking groups and events taking place in your vicinity. The longer the list, the better.
- Mark the entrance costs and the participants' description, as available to you.
- Are there any admission conditions? In addition, would you be able to present your business to the entire audience?

- How much time is dedicated to mingling?
- Last but not least, do you have a friend that is a part of that group or event, who is able to identify people that respond to your pre-classified targeted collaborators?

If so, it is recommended to learn why your friend believes that person is a good match for you, what their hobbies are and personal characteristics.

Go over the list and remove any low-grade event. A low-grade event or a low-grade networking group does not have the attendants you are looking for. A group of academics may include several clients for the cosmetic products. However, there is lower probability of locating two hair designers at such an event. On the other hand, an annual hair designer's competition may provide no clients but is the best place to pitch for potential collaborations.

The secret to successful business building via networking, lies in better preparation. Note that the right event for one business may be the wrong event for a different business owner. Setting your personal networking mission is the key.

Self-Presentation That Leads to a Paying Customer

You get three seconds. A goldfish has the memory span of eight seconds. A person in the 21st century has the attention span of THREE seconds.

Remember the elevator pitch model? Forget it. Remember the one-minute presentation model? Forget it.

Collaborate for Success

In today's world, where we are bombarded with advertisements all day long, our brain has developed new barriers instead of having to identify the lion in the woods for our fleeing instinct to rise, take over our brain and get us running. Our new instinct to flee, in this era, now rises when we sense an advertisement coming. A research conducted by Facebook and Nielsen Global Media found that after three seconds, around half the viewers lost interest, while out of the remaining viewers, around three quarters remained attentive for the coming ten seconds.

Once we accept that as a fact, our marketing strategy has to account for that client behavior in media production, which would be translated to visual, sound, bold heading and so on. In new age marketing language, that is called "the hook." Taken from the sport of fishing, you need to place the relevant hook for the specific type of fish you are aiming for. The same applies to marketing; you need to place the right hook to grab the specific, ideal customer's attention, which is in the first three seconds. Once the client is hooked, you have another few seconds to lure them in, which is the time span up to the ten-second mark. If they remain interested and responsive, then (and only then) they would indulge you with a full minute of attention. Once you have crossed that barrier successfully, and the potential client is still attending and responsive, then you may proceed with your short presentation of your service's or product's abilities.

True, these statistics are describing our attention to social media and the digital media. However, people are people, and if your client's attention span has been shortened to three seconds while playing with their beloved smartphone, consider that maybe you get an even shorter hooking time!

Going back to the networking mission, we set to attract at least two people who work, serve or sell products to our ideal clients.

We aim to hook them and offer a collaboration so that from now on they will send our ideal customers toward our business door. Reading the above, our task just became more complicated. That complication has two practical implications on your business. The first implication is that you need to make better preparations. There is a need to know and practice exactly how to identify the relevant people, and how to conduct ourselves during these first 3, 10, and 60-second introduction games. The second implication is that most of your competitors will not invest the required preparation time, leaving all the networking fruits ripe for you to collect.

The guarded secret of successful marketing is to accept that the client has no interest in you, your service or your product. As an entrepreneur who invested all their time and efforts in establishing their reputation, this may be a painful lesson. I urge you to rip the bandage fast, and accept that as soon as possible. The only interest the client has, focuses on solving their problems. That is true not only for your clients. It is also true regarding the people attending the networking event. These people all come to better their business, not to listen how they can better your business activity.

Here is a list of steps to solve all the above hurdles, hook the potential collaborator and lead your counterparty to invest a longer amount of time in listening to your pitch, while attending to their interest to better their business, and leading you toward accomplishing your mission statement, to better your business with a new flow of clients.

Starting with the correct dress code, the dress code has to fulfill two tasks. The first is to attest to your profession and what clients you are serving. The second is to attest that you understand the environment, and not come in shorts to a business mingling event. In one business conference where some three hundred professionals were practicing their mingling abilities, all were dressed nicely and were searching for business opportunities. One lady came dressed in a white Tuscany dress. Not only did she stand out from the crowd of business people, it was clear from her appearance that her business was organizing relaxation seminars. Her appearance was not only serving as a business card; it was also serving as a screening mechanism. People that were interested in that activity would approach, while the rest, who were not her targeted audience, would not, making her mingling and networking time more specific and successful. The business owner branding starts with their appearance and the clothing choices they make.

During the networking event, the first task is to identify the right person you believe may become a good collaborator. You may collect that information from a friend who can point you toward such an individual, or you may ask people in the room if they are a real estate agent, hair stylist, parent, instructor and so on. Once you identify the targeted person, your three seconds start.

First stage – Create an emotional connection. For example, state, "I help young moms, and I believe you work with the same audience." Such an opening gets the listener intrigued. They would want to know if you are a new competitor or a complementary service. They are probably consumed with their clients' behaviors, so they will have to give you some time to elaborate. Another alternative could emerge by talking about a joint hobby you and the listener have. Talking about hobbies is always a good relationship builder, though it may require a higher degree of homework preparation.

Second stage – Clearly demonstrate how you solve their burning problem. "I help young moms get their babies relaxed and fall asleep faster. I believe we can collaborate and better the lives of our clients together." Note that I immediately grab their attention with a specific client specification, and a specific client problem. If they serve those clients, then that would correspond with them immediately, and I would have touched on their main need: to better their clients' lives. It is safe to assume that they came to the networking event to locate clients and opportunities. Therefore, mentioning that we can serve their clients together, would get them thinking about collaborations immediately.

Third stage – Get them interested in taking action right now. "I believe our services/products are complementary to the same audience, and therefore a collaboration between us will achieve higher client affiliation, bringing more business to both of us." A bold approach would immediately reveal if that person can appreciate the collaboration logic or not. Their business may be in a different stage in the business life cycle and, hence, they are not open for anything, and discovering that sooner is an important time saver. Thus, if they came to the networking event to better their flow of clients, you would get them hooked.

Fourth stage – Detail what your rapport is like with their market niche. "I change these mom's lives in just two weeks, and I also believe bringing such assistance to your old clients will strengthen their connection to your business." Always state the gain their business will achieve from your activity. Yes, your listener would like to understand what it is you do, and how you better the lives of your clients, but as stated above, they are mainly interested in their own pain.

Bonus stage – By now, your pitch may go in two directions. Your listener may wish to continue with your discussion as they see the potential, or they may clearly state that they are not interested. In both scenarios, your bonus is to end this short meeting with a client referral. In both cases, you can proceed with, "Right now, do you have one or two people, friends or young moms that you think may benefit from talking to me?" It is probable that in both scenarios, you will receive a referral. In case that person may wish to set a future meeting to explore your collaboration offer, they would be glad to demonstrate their good intentions; while if they have no interest in progressing toward a collaboration, they would probably also wish to show their appreciation for your ability to serve their clients.

You have just changed the networking game board, from a fisherman's behavior—spreading business cards or giving a one-minute presentation on stage, and hoping relevant clients will approach you—to a hunter's behavior, targeting a specific, relevant person, and aiming at setting such a collaboration that would continuously point the ideal customers toward your front door, or at least get a referral to two specific clients immediately.

Note that mastering such a technique may require some practice; however, it can lead to approaching two to four potential collaborators in each networking event.

Chapter 10

Laser Point Your Client to Increase Your Profits

> *"Our success as a global brand has been directly related to how we select locations where we are confident our particular clients desire to be."*
> – Anthony Hitt

Between Target Market and an Ideal Customer

For many years, the main role of the marketing team was to identify and investigate the relevant target market for the company's products and services, with the purpose of making sure your service correlates with the market needs. The marketing role is to conduct a careful analysis of the competition, demographics, segmentation, positioning and so on. The intention of that exercise is to make sure the marketing budget gets the brand exposure at the best places, in front of the target market, whilst also assisting the sales efforts and making the life of the salesperson easier. In any business course, it is taught that the target market is the description of the range of people or businesses at which you aim your marketing efforts so that they will buy your product or service.

Focusing on the target market is a continuous process: visiting both the audience and the company's developing team to make sure the product is aligned with the market's needs. As market trends change, the marketing role is to revert that feedback to the development team so that the product or service will be updated to resonate with the new market needs and trends.

The marketing will bring one of the company's products or services forward. Though a company may have a variety of products or services, the marketing plan will only focus its budget on one, and that is true and valid for all organizations of any size, for the simple reason that no one has enough marketing budget to offer all their products at all times. Let us take as an example a large enough organization, one that we can assess is spending greater amounts on marketing than you are able to. Let us talk about Coca Cola, can we agree their marketing budget is greater?! Please close your eyes and try to guess how many products their full catalogue presents (different SKU)? Now, try recalling how many of their products you have seen on the media?

I can guess the later response is around 2-3 products, probably Coke, Sprite and maybe diet or zero products. The number of SKU's they produce is over 3,500! But we see adds for only two to three because even they do not have large enough marketing budget to market all products to all markets, they also focus their investment. While also focusing the marketing investment on specific target audience, even though every person may like soft drinks. They chose to focus their efforts to a target market of young active youth.

In recent years, something has changed. The change started some decades ago while exposing us to an overload of TV commercials. However the advertisements explosion came with the internet and social media commercial activity. Back in the 70's the average consumer in the U.S. was exposed to around 500 ads per day. That number has since increased greatly. According to Forbs, estimations are that most Americans are exposed to around 4,000 to 10,000 ads each day. Implication is simple, clients have developed a screening process. We activate our primal fight-or-flight instinct, and we flee from anything that just appears to be an advertisement.

Combining the two above-mentioned factors. First is the limited marketing budget and second is the client flee instinct. Resulted in a new marketing perception. A new level of focus was born, the identification of the ideal client. No longer can we set the marketing towards a large target market, as they flee. We now have to identify a specific individual whom would benefit the most of our service or product, and target them specifically.

The logic leading to the development of that approach is that once a person feels that the marketing is communicating with their specific need, the barrier will be lowered and they will respond. Being able to talk directly to a specific person bypasses the automatic advertisement blocking-screen. Remember, their attention span is also tree seconds.

Here are the main criteria for choosing the ideal customer:

Market size - it is advisable to choose a large and renewable target audience over a niche audience.

Economic indicators - it is advisable to choose a target audience whose economic situation allows purchasing the product with a relative ease, than one how would need to invest their last few pennies for that purchase.

Characterization of the customer - the potential customer has to be identified, their needs and their preferences exposed.

After the general characterization of the potential customers, we will go back and emphasize that you are not capable (And in fact, no business can) of advertising all products to all customers.

The right way is to choose one customer, a single person to be very specific, and directing all our attention to that specific person. While at the end of the sale process, we may be able to present that customer with additional products and expand sales towards them. However, at first stage we need to gain their trust and turn them from a potential customer into a paying customer.

To conclude, in order for your marketing effort to bear fruit, it must focus on a particular customer and offer a particular product.

Determine Avatar/ Ideal Customer Characteristics

The origin of the word comes from the Hindu language. "Avatar" means "revelation" with the borrowed religious meaning of the "descent" of God from heaven to earth and his incarnation in a specific historical figure.

The term Avatar has migrated out of Indian and religious space and was borrowed to the world of marketing. The term is now used to denote the representation of a particular customer.

True, your business has a story based on you and the vision for which you set up the business. You have already set your business values or you may have decided to offer your audience with the products you produce. However, in order of attracting the right customers for you, you are required to place the customer at the center your business. In other words, the customer's needs will define your marketing and sales strategy and not the vision for which you set up the business.

Therefore, our goal in building your client's avatar is to allow you to get into their shoes. See the world from their unique point of view, and from that viewpoint you will later understand their difficulties and needs and why your product may help them overcome their difficulties.

As mentioned above, the marketing base should not focus on convincing the customer to purchase the product. It should be focused on providing the customer with the product they require in order of solve a problem that is bothering them.

As an example, a good salesperson may be able to sell ice to one or two Eskimos, but a smart salesperson will sell coats to more Eskimos and with greater ease. Seeing your customer's needs, the needs of the same person that you defined earlier, is the backbone of the whole sales process, and ultimately only the understanding of the customer's needs will create sales.

As Brian Clark, an entrepreneur and the founder of Copyblogger, said, *"You don't just accept who you find—you choose who to attract."*

Your ability to understand the client will allow you to grab the customer's attention. When the client sees that you know them, and that you know how to solve the exact problem they are suffering from, then you have opened the door to their attention.

Therefore, we do not talk to an audience, but only with the exact avatar or ideal customer. Later on, it is okay to define several different ideal customers.

Your financial success hides behind the amount of time and thought that will be invested in researching that ideal client.

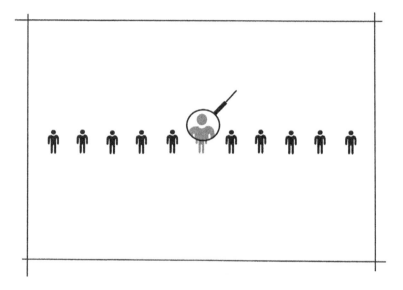

In determining your avatar's characteristics, consider and identify the following details:

Profession and occupation – Detail what the avatar does and what work/family decisions they influence.

Demographics – Revive the avatar as an individual. What is their age, gender, income level, education, marital status and where he or she lives?

Psychography – Get into your avatar's head: What hobbies do they hold? What are their life values? What approach do they take, and what are their interests?

Goals, Challenges and Difficulties – What is their main purpose? What stands in their way? What holds them back from fulfilling their purpose, and what keeps them awake at night?

Objections and Their Role in the Purchase Process – Why would your ideal customer not buy from you, and how much influence does that person have over the buying decision?

Media use – From where does your avatar get their information? Note specific websites, their favorite books, news sources and other sources.

Investigate Your Ideal Customer

An established business would most commonly possess a good understanding of its ideal client. However, the depth of research and resources invested in investigating the chosen ideal customer will determine how easy the sales process will be.

The ability to deeply understand the ideal customer is probably the most important action you would ever make in your business marketing strategy planning. Only if you know exactly who you want your marketing to target, can you construct a message that will hit the potential client straight in the stomach.

Once you manage to construct a message that reports to the inner conversation taking place in your client's mind, they would react immediately. The potential client will inevitably feel that you are aware of their difficulties and pains, and if you are, then it would also imply that you have the knowledge and the ability to solve these pains, leading the client to the inevitable reaction that would influence the business bottom line. That is, to order the product or service offered. Never forget that your clients have many options of where to spend their hard-earned money, and all alternatives offer great solutions; however, only a few manage to get the client to feel he is understood, and our objective is to convey that message.

It is advisable to start by conducting deep level interviews with existing and potential clients. Where possible, it is advisable to ask permission and record such interviews. Reasoning for these recordings will be discussed in the coming pages, while right now we shall focus on the data collection guidelines and what information is better collected.

- For basic understanding, interview 6–10 clients; for a deeper understanding, interview up to 10% of the business customer list.

- Interview colleagues; ask for the customer questions they face, what objections they experience and how they respond to their customers.

- Ask your customers what features of your products or services they like, what bothers them and what needs to be improved.

- Conduct an online survey, using the tools available on Google, Facebook, etc.

- Examine your clients' customer behavior on your business website and social media pages.

- Use available tools like Google Analytics, and relevant available tools like Facebook, Twitter, YouTube, Pinterest and so on.

- If you have previously used email campaigns, analyze which campaigns were more successful, and identify what differences were visible between the different campaigns. Was it in the wording, in the pictures, in the media used?

After examination of the business internal information, set out to explore the ideal customer behavior as it manifests elsewhere. Use Google Search Console to gather insights relating to what questions, challenges and problems your audience faces. This tool shows you which questions were asked by these people and to which of your website pages they were referred.

Examine the competitors' social media channels. Look for their customers' demographic and psychographic characteristics. Identify serial responders and try characterizing them personally. Read relevant blogs and pay special attention to the questions and comments raised by readers in the comments.

Further insights could be found at Amazon. People tend to respond and detail their thoughts in respect to books they have read. As our goal is to collect our audience's thoughts and language patterns, this is a great source for insights. Identify books that deal with the same pains you know your clients are facing, and read the reviews, focusing only on the high (5-star) reviews and the low (1-star) reviews. That is where you will find the emotions. Reviews like, "The thing I liked most about this book was..." or "I disliked the book because..." provide great understanding of the clients. The reviews will reveal the clients' sophistication level: Do they only look for new developments, or are they happy with old systems that work just as well? Are they happy to share personal information? Have they received that book as a gift, or invested in themselves? And so on.

Register Your Findings

Now comes the fun stage of writing each avatar's story. This is the time to connect the dots and produce a uniform story, a portrait of the avatar. First, draft the story, and then to revive the avatar, select a name for him or her, match a stock image to represent the character, and prepare a background story describing the motivation and goals that guide your avatar.

Even though, as an established business, you already know your customers' needs and characteristics, it is safe to assume that some new, interesting and even surprising facts have been revealed during that avatar construction exercise.

It is possible that from your new, more detailed acquaintance with the ideal customer, you suddenly discovered that their other family members are also prospective clients of your products or services, thus increasing your potential market share at no extra cost.

On the next page is a worksheet template for the avatar personality registration. A digital worksheet is also available on my website at www.CollaborateSuccess.com.

Laser Point Your Client to Increase Your Profits

Ideal Customer Overview

A. Personal description

1. Are they a man or a woman?
2. What is their age?
3. What is their marital status?
4. How many children do they have?
5. What is their place of residence?
6. Choose a name: _____ (e.g., Danny the programmer, Dian the CEO, Liz the athlete)
7. What is their physical structure (weight, hair color, eye color, etc.)?
8. What is their appearance (clothing, style, level of personal care, etc.)?
9. What hobbies do they have?
10. What does he/she do in their spare time?
11. What is their occupation? (Be as accurate as possible.)
12. What is their annual income?
13. What is their level of education?
14. What are the values that are most important to them?

B. Mental state (fears and aspirations)

15. What is he/she afraid of?
    Fear is what keeps us awake at night! What are they deeply afraid of (work relationships, personal relationships, career, etc.)?
    Make a list of fears (5–6 fears) and a list of concerns (5–6 concerns).
16. What do they wish would happen to them as a result of using the product or service?
    What aspirations and imaginings do they see in their mind?

C. Language and way of expression

17. Identify and write down the words used by them to describe their main problem or need. These are available via a social networks search, Amazon search and the recorded interviews. It is probable that the words used by the clients are different from the way you describe the exact same thing. Note their terminology.

D. The sales process

18. Where does the ideal customer get the information relating to their problem (books, sites, events, celebrities, etc.)?
19. What are the objections you discovered?
(Detail 3–5 objections.)
20. What are your responses to these objections?

Calibrate Your Marketing with the Client's Desires and Needs

"Life is an ongoing process of choosing between safety (out of fear and need for defense) and risk (for the sake of progress and growth). Make the growth choice a dozen times a day."
– Abraham Maslow

Setting the right collaboration is the shortcut to multiplying the word-of-mouth recommendation approach to gaining clients, and is the step forward from real clients' recommendations into a system providing ongoing exposure to the ideal customers as defined by each business. However, that does not mean we neglect our clients' power to act as our best marketing people. Happy clients are probably the most important asset of any successful business. Providing clients with great results is obviously the base for any measure of client satisfaction. However, just as important is the ease they experience while shifting from their initial skeptic mindset to that purchasing action, leading them to use the product or to experience the service provided.

Shifting a person from exploring a purchase opportunity, to the real life usage of a product or service, should not only concentrate on getting the deal done. If one of our business missions states that we aim to please our clients in a way that they will become part of our marketing and brand exposure strategy, then we are confronted with the task of bonding the client with our brand and product. Creating this bond starts the minute the potential client is exposed to the product, and not only after they have used it and are happy with the results achieved.

Controlling the client's brand interaction experience starts with understanding that person's mental state in relation to their relevant problem, the same problem that our product is aiming to solve. It is our task to understand our customers, because only they can help us get more leads and more business. Understanding the product influence with the customers is the key to giving them good service, which in turn leads to strong customer relationships, and only then will we accomplish our mission of getting new sales through positive word-of-mouth recommendations. Earlier, we invested in studying the specific ideal customer in depth. We have asked for their fears and their hardships. Now it is time to place these in context so that our conversation with the client will lead to faster sales, while also making sure that the client feels they fulfilled their needs.

Maslow's hierarchy of needs was developed by the psychologist Abraham Maslow, in the 1940s, and has since been used to explain human behavior. It is also widely used by marketers to explain what motivates consumers to behave as they do.

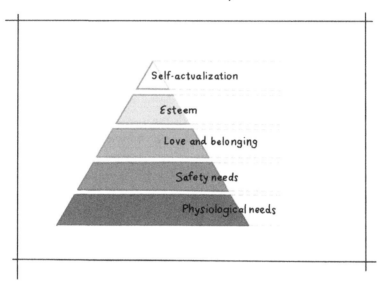

Maslow described five stages of needs in hierarchical order:

Physiological Needs – referring to the basics of food, water, clothing and shelter.

Safety and Security – referring to health, employment, housing, family and social stability.

Love and Belonging – referring to friendships, family life, intimacy and a sense of connection.

Self-Esteem – referring to feelings of confidence, achievement and gaining respect from others.

Self-Actualization – referring to moral standing, creativity, spontaneity, having a purpose and maximizing inner potential.

Maslow's claim is that as people meet the needs of each level, they move toward accomplishing and fulfilling their needs as described at the next level and so on. For a business, it is important to understand which of these needs are fulfilled by their product or service. A food business could be offering bread and butter, fulfilling clients' basic physiological needs. However, a food business could also be offering Michelin three-star gourmet catering, thus fulfilling the diners' fourth level of self-esteem and achievement needs. Understanding the effect your product has on the client's need, includes contemplating its effect on their overall life needs, not only the specific need the product corresponds to.

Earlier, we used the second-hand car sales negotiation for the purpose of identifying the interests each person had toward the transaction. We noted that one was aiming to cover a loan, which corresponds to Maslow's second level of security; while paying for the daughter's wedding may respond to the fulfillment of the third level, by taking care of the family. The buyer was interested in getting a safe family car with a spacious rear seat for the children, corresponding to Maslow's second level by providing security and taking care of the family's safety needs. Since you are reading this book, we can assume you are aiming at fulfilling your personal and business growth at the higher levels of the pyramid.

In the developed countries of today's modern world, it is reasonable to assess that most businesses deal with clients that are not hungry for food as a basic physiological level. Thus, the interaction with the client or your collaboration partner does not need to focus on fulfilling their basic needs. It should communicate with their desires to climb to the higher level of self-esteem and self-actualization. The feeling we want our client or collaborator to feel is that due to collaborating with our business, or due to using our product or service, they will climb faster toward self-actualization. Using our marketing tools, we need to inspire our ideal customer or our collaboration partner. Our mission is to convey a message of growth rather than of basic needs fulfillment.

Consider how Coca Cola does not state, "We provide a drink so that you stay dehydrated." The Coca Cola slogan progressed from "Thirst knows no season" (1922), referring to the basic physiological need, to "Life tastes good" (2001), referring to the product's taste at the lower physical levels, while also looking higher up to "life is good." The slogan then moved to "Together tastes better" (2020), referring to the higher level of belonging to a group and being together; while in some territories, they progressed to "Love the life," hinting that with their product, you reach the highest level of life actualization.

The marketing purpose is also to engage in that internal discussion with the client's mind, leading them to experience growth from the minute they engage with your brand, rather than waiting until they experience the wonderful results the product or service has provided them.

Talk the Talk

Communication skills are noted particularly when exploring international trade. We all know that doing business in Japan or in Greece would require a different business behavior. However, the same importance should be granted to the daily communication any business conducts with its customers. We have earlier discussed the calibration of the business to that of the customers' needs. Now let us note that the customer will pronounce their needs in a certain manner. The language the customer uses to pronounce their needs and interests is not a simple verbal expression. People correlate the words they choose with what goes on inside their head, and the customer is not an exception. When conducting the avatar research, I advised you to ask permission to record the interviews. The importance of that recording is discussed at this stage. We are aware that customers have developed a salesperson barrier: Anything that sounds like a product push is blocked as soon as possible. Our business intention is not only to gain more customers, but rather to have happy customers that experience an emotional connection to our brand.

The emotional connection is best created through the calibration of the brand's language patterns with those of the ideal customer's. An energy bar producer may offer a "banana flavored energy bar." That could well be a true description of the product. However, if their ideal customers are school kids that would eat these bars during their morning break, a better product description could be "the 10 o'clock snack." And if we were offering the same product to professional athletes, we may choose to call it "the high energy and carbs supplement"—same product, different descriptions, aimed at creating rapport with different avatars.

When aiming at creating better rapport with the ideal customer, there is a need to adopt their language patterns (i.e. communicate with their inner thoughts). It is easy to understand that professional athletes would use different language patterns than schoolchildren; however, with our clients, it is a more complex situation. Any business that is aiming for a specific market segment, there is an ongoing interaction with the clientele, and there is a belief that we know the clients' needs just as well as they do. Unfortunately, that is not enough if we aim to create a connection with the customer's inner thoughts even before they place the order. The right way to connect with their inner thoughts is by talking their talk—using their exact words.

While researching the avatar, we registered—or even better, recorded—their fears, pains and interests. We now understand that we were not only interested in what they were saying but also in how they were saying it. What were their exact words? The specific words they used to describe their fears and needs would facilitate the marketing efforts from start to finish. There is a need to use the ideal customer's exact words when making the ads, while conducting the sales dialogue and when opening the road for a new collaboration.

People respond better to their peers. Thus, while offering your service or product, you aspire for your customer to consider your brand as their peer. The client would always respond better to a salesperson that seems to understand their specific situation and needs. Those needs are pronounced only by their specific words.

A further advantage you can achieve when listening to and learning from the recordings, lies with the subtext. The subtext is like the "thinking bubbles" that reveal a character's thoughts in comics. Picking up on your customer's subtext requires some practice, but it is the fastest way to a deeper relationship. Consider what you actually hear when your spouse or child responds to you that they are "fine," when you know they are not. Listening to the same recording, several times, will reveal some deep subtext that would provide a high-end marketing advantage.

Practically speaking, the customer's language should be used to achieve the following three goals:

- Attract your ideal customer (the avatar) and establish an emotional connection with them.
- Show the customers in clear words how you can solve their burning problem.

- Stimulate a desire to take action, whether it is to contact you, purchase from you or any action relevant to the service you are providing.

Strategize Your Path to Your Ideal Customer's Heart

Interesting and important fact: Only 5% of the customers who meet your product information will make a purchase during or following the first exposure. Writing nice and targeted texts would not solve all your marketing problems. As mentioned, during the current age of information overflow, our brain works as a fine filter. Therefore, it is assumed with high probability that during the first customer encounter with your site or post or ad, no purchase will be made. The way to deal with the automatic filtering that runs in their head is to make sure they will meet you and your brand over and over again, until the relationship is established and they perform the purchase.

The way to perform that task is called a marketing funnel. The sales funnel is a figurative image of the client's path, from the moment they are first exposed to a product or a brand, up until they perform the purchase. In the old days, before online measurement tools, that task was less complicated but also less effective. At first, a brand would set their mass exposure via TV, newspaper or radio ads. The second exposure would be set up at the shop entrance or next to the shelves and so on. The idea was to expose as many people to the first ad, knowing that only a very small portion of the public are real potential customers. Some would then walk to the shop and be exposed to the second level advertisement, and an even smaller portion of the public would take the route toward the shelves, and only then would they see that product marketing design.

At the top of the funnel are the general public, including many potential customers, and at the bottom are paying customers, those who are the real purpose of the sales process. At the bottom, we meet the people for whom the business was established.

In the current social media and search engine era, the funnel has become much more sophisticated, enabling precise measurement of each client's activity at any stage of their purchase process. Though this may sound deterring, the implication is that the marketing activities are much more affordable, and any small business is now able to perform marketing activities that once were only available to the largest multinationals. Knowing the business-specific ideal customer allows any business to focus all their marketing investment directly toward these potential clients—those with the highest need for the product—and they provide the highest sales opportunities and higher chances for client satisfaction.

Nevertheless, the number of people that are exposed to your site is significantly greater than the amount of customers who will purchase the product or your service. The marketing wisdom focuses on the client path. That is the process the client goes through, from the moment of their exposure to the product, to when they develop the product awareness, to when their interest is raised, and to resolving objections and eventually taking action and making the purchase.

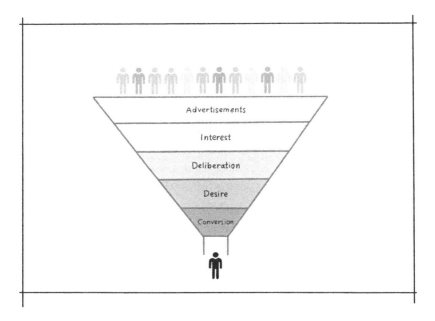

Advertisements – The wide side of the funnel, the target audience and the ideal customer are exposed to the brand's information through external links, sponsored advertising, social media, etc.

Interest – The ideal customer visits your site as a result of advertising or conducting their own organic search at Google, looking for your product. At this stage, we respond to the customer's interest while providing detailed information and elaborating around the product or service's advantages to the ideal customer, in their own words.

Deliberation – The interested person now becomes a potential customer. They will compare the product or service to competing products in order to maximize the result from their investment, and to get the "best value for their money." That does not mean that they will look for the cheapest product; rather, they would search for the product that will best respond to their needs and provide them with highest satisfaction. It is therefore important to present the product by using their words in a way that will lead the ideal customer toward the next step.

Conversion – Your ideal customer is now performing the desired action, as determined by you. That could be purchasing the product, picking up the phone to make an appointment, etc.

A similar funnel should be designed when attempting to cause another person to join in a collaboration with your business. There is a need to study their professional language, to understand the names and adjectives that are used by professionals of their trade. Then design a dedicated funnel, where you walk that potential collaborator through the stages of exposing your business and intentions: advertisement stage. Arouse their interest toward the prospect of collaborating with your business: interest stage. Provide information that would respond to any of their expected concerns and fears, while also listening to their interests: deliberation stage. Finally, determine the collaboration's objectives, designate roles and tasks, and launch it to the world: conversion stage.

ACKNOWLEDGEMENTS

A few years back, I took the mission of interpreting business practices and procedures commonly used by the larger organizations, to micro businesses of one to ten persons, businesses that are struggling under their own business operations. I see this book as a collection and summary of negotiation practices, packed into a simple-to-practice model that could be utilized by any business owner. As I look at the process of bringing this book to life, I would like to acknowledge the many people who accompanied me along the way; some as business partners who joined me in different ventures, others from whom I have learned by observation, and the people that caused that know-how to be collected and transferred onto these pages.

First, my family, of course. Starting with my parents, **Dina** and **Dr. Uri,** for accompanying me through my life's journey since it began, enabling my diverse explorations with support that is quite extraordinary and for exampling a life of fulfillment and good-doing.

To my loved son-in-law, **Ariel,** and my children, **Shaked, Tomer,** and **Chen,** , who have chosen to join my adventures through good times and lesser times. I am honored to observe these young adults demonstrating a life of social contribution. Each of them is a leader, and each is embarking on their life journey with determination and confidence. I am appreciative of your role and your presence in my journey.

Collaborate for Success

To my dear friends, who are like family, **Noory and Bella Fisher,** parents to First-Lieutenant **Avi Fisher** KIA, my best friend who was killed while fighting terror. I would like to thank them for their life example of how it is possible to live through hardships while growing an amazing family.

To my friend and mentor, **Kane Minkus,** an extraordinary entrepreneur and the founder of Industry Rockstar, who came into my life just a few years ago. With the blink of an eye, he spotlighted a path that eventually led to the birth of this book. And to **Alessia Minkus** and all the iR team for their exemplary team work and dedication. On top of all, I would like to add a special thanks and acknowledgment to Kane for investing his valuable time towards writing the introduction to this book.

To **Kathy Ireland,** a unique person, a business mogul, for showing kindness to all and making it a point to create that personal connection that leads to success. And to **Jason Winters,** Vision Strategist and co-founder at Kathy Ireland Worldwide, for their large scale marketing world view, and for their trust in the Israeli market, and faith in setting a collaboration with myself. To **Thomas Meharey,** Vice President, and **Bialik Benjamin,** V.P. of Business Development, for proving grand organizations can show flexibility while partnering and collaborating with SMBs. To that great team for demonstrating how a world leading organization can take a hands-on approach for the benefit of its clients, and for showing flexibility and availability aimed at making each client feel they are important.

To my mentor, **Kevin Harrington,** the entrepreneur's entrepreneur, the inventor of the infomercial, and the "original shark" on Shark Tank, also known as the 6-billion-dollar guy, for his accessibility and assistance in bettering my work processes.

Acknowledgements

To **Kevin Paetz,** a great entrepreneur who is also leading several companies. A leader of people from whom I had the privilege of learning some high end management secrets. I would like to thank Kevin for dedicating his precious time to the benefit of this book.

To my friend and business partner, **Athanasion Koutsogiotas,** AKA **Sakis,** for demonstrating how people can connect via a simple collaboration to become life friends and business partners, for his honest opinion at any business deliberation, and for demonstrating great abilities in the negotiation rooms.

To **Yossi Solnik,** my former business partner that became a life friend, for teaching me how friendship could be built based on mutual life goals, and how friends can manage a business and even dissolve it while remaining good friends, and for joining me in a quest to better the lives of patients and becoming a role model for easy going negotiation practices.

To **Alan Schwartz,** Executive Vice President of mdi Consultants, for his friendship and trust, for providing backing and assistance in launching an innovative service for SMBs, and for demonstrating that the right collaboration may last for long years and provide clients with best results.

To **Benzion Geshuri,** an entrepreneur and a visionary, and Dr. **Raanan Geshuri,** CEO of Keshet Prima, for their joint trust and opening the door for me to their fortress, allowing me to join and observe how a large scale industrial organization can demonstrate flexibility and set ongoing collaborations and partnerships at grand scale.

Finally, to the people that brought this book into existence:

To **Raymond Aaron,** my publisher and the moving force behind this book. He is Canada's number one success and investment coach, an author of over 140 books, and a *New York Times* top-10 best-selling author. He took an idea and turned it into reality with a magic wand. And to all the team at 10-10-10 Publishing, and especially **Liz Ventrella**, **Waqas Chaudhry, Christina Fife** and **Lisa Browning** for guiding the birth of this book, proofing this manuscript and bringing it to life.

Last but not least, to the great designers that took part in bringing this book to life, **Leni Smolovich** of **Studio Leni Graphics,** a friend and a great collaborator that rolled up her sleeves and designed the great cover for this book. And **Dana Bender,** a talented artist and a soon-to-be architect, for freeing some time in her hectic schedule and illustrating this book.

To all those friends and teachers along the path of my life—too many to mention—whose strategies, insights and examples I had the honor to observe and learn from. I give thanks to you all and hope I can live up to the task of passing that collective knowledge onward.

ABOUT THE AUTHOR

Gilad Segev is a leading expert in establishing income-generating collaborations.

Gilad is an entrepreneur and a mentor. He is an attorney and holds an MBA in international trade. He is an arbitrator and a certified mediator. Since 2006, his office has been accompanying manufacturing companies to break into international markets, while mentoring freelancers and small businesses to increase business revenue and reach stabilization, using his unique techniques.

Gilad is an expert in the WIN/WIN negotiating technique, bringing over 20 years of diverse managerial experience, during which he was employed in senior management positions in a variety of industries. Amongst them, he served as CEO of a financing company, CEO of a medical device company, VP of finance, international marketing manager, sales manager and more. That unique variety of positions allows him a unique organizational point of view that helps his clients identify and define problems and tailor creative solutions.

According to Gilad, *"I see a mission in changing the situation, whereby the chances of a visionary who has taken the initiative and set up a business, eventually experiences difficulty making a living, supporting his family, and bringing their personal vision into the world."*

Gilad spends his free time between the sea and the desert, and makes sure to fuel his mind and soul with voluntary activities.

He is a sought after speaker and an occasional writer.

MEET THE AUTHOR, COLLECT THE BONUSES AND MORE, AT
www.CollaborateSuccess.com.

BONUSES AND TOOLS

Bonuses are available for you at
www.CollaborateSuccess.com.

Bonus 1 – Negotiations conclusion-drawing guide

Bonus 2 – List of 36 places for locating potential collaborators

Made in the USA
Monee, IL
21 December 2021